JET SMART

FL\

Maui

1992

JET SMART

Copyright © 1992 by Diana Fairechild

First Printing, July 1992
Second Printing, October 1992, revised

All rights reserved. The author of this book does not dispense medical advice nor prescribe the use of any technique as a form of treatment for medical problems without the advice of a physician, either directly or indirectly. The intent of the author is only to offer information of a general nature. In the event you use information from this book for yourself, you are prescribing for yourself. The author/publisher assumes no responsibility.

Written permission must be obtained prior to commercial use. Parts of this book, up to 300 words, may be reproduced without permission for personal use if the names of author/publisher are clearly stated with the reproduction. All inquiries/comments/suggestions should be addressed to the publisher:

FLYANA RHYME Inc - PO Box 300
Makawao, Maui, Hawaii 96768 - USA
Tel/FAX 808.572.5252

Editors: Richard Joseph Lafond Jr. and Paul Wood
Illustrations: Bart Goldman
Cover art: Donn DeShayne
Layout design: Patt Narrowe
Photo: Patt Narrowe and Richard Joseph Lafond Jr.

Library of Congress Cataloging in Publication Data
Fairechild, Diana
JET SMART
    Bibliography:p.
    Includes index.
1. Jet Lag   2. Environmental Health   3. Travel – Health Aspects.   4. Flight – Physiological Aspects.   5. Naturopathy.

Printed in the United States of America
LC 92-73279
ISBN 0-9630198-0-5

TABLE OF CONTENTS

Stalking the Dragon

ACKNOWLEDGEMENTS

JET SMART evolved like one of those big picture puzzles — tiny piece by piece. The whole has only now revealed itself. First there were writing inspirations, then research discoveries, editorial polishes, publication decisions, cover and layout designs, and, finally, financing. In addition to the artists credited on the title page, I want to acknowledge the following friends for their help and support.

Each person listed on this page offered a unique, precious piece to the JET SMART puzzle — everything from inspirations to IBM compatibles (three over the last fourteen years). To describe the behind-the-scenes her-story in its entirety would require another book. For now, all I can do is to simply say, thank you.

Steve Bellamy
John Bremmer
Mary Broeringmeyer, D.C.
Susie Bryson
Ron Carlson
John Cogan, M.D.
Darla Curry
Sondra Edwards
Charlie Elias
Elizabeth Elliott
Jim Fahey
Diana Finch
Lynn Gillen
Linda Glas
Jerry Herbert
Helen Hite
Pamela Hoey

Jonny Johnson
Robert Keilbach
Chris & Kurt Koller
Sandi Langlais
Joan Ocean
Pearl Orenstein
Marcia Pearlman
Dee Pollock
M.A. Quest
Roy Rowan
Peter Sanford
Robbie Sherson
Maggie Stanford
Buff Thompson
Bertil Werjefelt
Dove White

*To the world's
flight attendants*

I have literally circled the planet over 100 times. If you add up all the miles I've flown, though, it's more like 300 orbits.

Working as an international flight attendant offered me a unique perspective in which to assess the effects of jetlag, to experiment with cures on flights and on layovers, and to seek out remedies all over the world. However, it wasn't until I was permanently medically grounded, after twenty-one years of nonstop jetlag, that I fully realized the importance of my years experience and research.

Throughout this book, whenever possible, significant research is cited, along with my own personal experience of wellness and my close observations of hundreds of thousands of human subjects — my passengers. You see, we have really served each other!

Wishing you all the joys of travel.

Happy landings,

DIANA FAIRECHILD

Meeting the Dragon

GOLDEN DAYS OF RADIO

AUSTRALIA $1

ONCE UPON A TIMEZONE

DRAGON BREATH (What Is Jetlag?)

Today, nonstop flights vault half the globe in airplanes longer from nose to tail than the entire distance covered by Orville Wright's first flight. Certainly Mr. Wright would shout with joy to see a modern 747. Even so, revving up on runways 'round the world, today's passengers must be asking themselves the same question raised by Wilbur and Orville back in 1903: *Will this thing really get off the ground?*

Although the technology of aircraft has vastly improved, the human experience of travel remains a challenging travail. And now, one billion of us fly annually. We jet with all convenient rapidity between high-ceilinged shrines to travel — airports — where huge timetables click off arrival/departure data in mesmerizing rhythm which mimics our fascination with speed.

The airlines formulate these timetables using "block time." The clock starts when wooden blocks (which keep a parked aircraft's wheels from rolling) are removed just prior to leaving a gate. The clock stops when a different set of blocks is shoved into place at an arrival airport.

Yet, as frequent flyers and crew know, jet travel consumes time and energy well beyond that between the blocks. For instance, a "typical flight attendant is on duty 3.5 hours for every one hour in the air."[1] And crew members, unlike most passengers, travel with relative efficiency: bypass airport check-in and baggage claim, shuttle via buses with special airport parking permits, and assemble at designated hotels.

For passengers, the difference between actual elapsed time and block time is greater still, comprising a long journey of seven stages:

1) Jet Prep: plan, ticket, pack.
2) Jet Ready: car/taxi/bus/rail to airport.
3) Jet Set: check-in, security, gate, wait.
4) Jet Go: enplane, taxi, flight, taxi, deplane.
5) Jet Down: immigration, customs, baggage claim.
6) Jet Let-Go: car/taxi/bus/rail away from airport.
7) Jetlag: coping with that taxing time warp.

Over 90% of jetters complain of physical and mental problems associated with long-distance travel — according to my own informal surveys taken during twenty-one years in perpetual orbit as an international flight attendant. Most people consider jet travel an occasionally pleasant, yet essentially tormenting necessity.

And, of all the challenges we travelers face — rising airfares, terrorism threats, security checks, congested airports, flight delays, crowded planes, airline meals, aging fleets, air traffic tangles, inclement weather, and jetlag — jetlag concerns people most, because it imposes itself on us long after our aircraft lands. From the practical point of view we cannot begin to estimate the consequences of errors of judgment, incapacitation, and increase in accident rates due to jetlag.[2]

Without a clear understanding of jetlag, travelers assume no responsibility for its control. As a result, attitudes of resignation, frustration, or even resentment further compound the jetlag ordeal.

This book offers a ray of hope to these weary flyers yearning to breathe free. Together, we will understand the mechanics of jetting and how our well-being — our bodies, minds, emotions, and even our spiritual outlook — is impacted by jet travel.

In the course of my research, I've collated a list of jetlag symptoms and have classified them into four categories: physical, mental, emotional, and spiritual jetlag.

Physical Jetlag. Activities at home, where we are normally adept, can be, after jetting, clumsily out of step. Greg Louganis was the first world-class athlete to publicly blame jetlag, after he accidentally hit his head on the diving platform at the '79 Olympic trials.[3] Today, international athletes regularly cite jetlag as the cause of impaired performances.

Physical Jetlag Symptoms:

body aches	irregular heartbeat
clammy sweat	lightheadedness
constipation	loss of sexual impetus
diarrhea	loss of grip strength
dry cough	low blood sugar
dry eyes	low energy
dry skin	modified reaction to drugs
earache	nausea
fatigue	nervous tension
headache	oversensitivity to pain
hemorrhoids	shallow breathing
impaired coordination	sore throat
impaired vision	susceptibility to illness
insomnia	swollen feet

Mental Jetlag. Diplomat John Foster Dulles blamed jetlag for the Suez Crisis in the fifties, when he was U.S. Secretary of State. Years later, Dulles confessed that heavy jetlag to and from Egypt had prevented him from thinking clearly.[4]

Mental Jetlag Symptoms:

disorientation	fear
distortion of time/distance	hallucination
inability to concentrate	memory loss

Emotional Jetlag. Inflight brawls over armrests,[5] passengers who refuse to follow instructions, passengers who vent their frustrations by assaulting flight attendants — these can be, and often are, examples of emotional jetlag. Jetlag appears to have the power to ignite the emotions of even the most ostensibly invulnerable people.

Emotional Jetlag Symptoms:

anxiety	indecisiveness
depression	insecurity
euphoria	irascibility
impatience	vulnerability

Spiritual Jetlag. In the rare atmosphere of jets passengers often feel an uncommon intensity and magnification of their faith in the Creator — or lack of it. Questions such as: *Will I die on this flight?* and *Why am I here?* are examples of the type of thinking which appears to regularly bubble up at higher altitudes.

Spiritual Jetlag Symptoms:

at-One-ness	at-numb-ness

When we jet, there are so many new sensations; at times, it is difficult to assess whether a symptom is specifically the result of jetlag or whether it has been caused by something else associated with air travel. For example, the symptom *dry cough*, when experienced by crew members on the higher-altitude polar flights, is commonly attributed to ozone exposure (page 68). *Impaired coordination* is a symptom I track back to north/south crossings (page 13), sleep deprivation after all nighters (page 35), and/or pesticide exposure on certain flights (page 90).

Obviously, a lot gets assimilated under the popular tag "jetlag." Some writers have even called the disorientation experienced by shift workers "jetlag without leaving home" or "industrial jetlag."

Jetlag is commonly spelled "jet lag" or "jet-lag" and you may have noticed that I have taken the liberty of removing the space or hyphen. In this jet age, jetlag is such a universal and common experience, it deserves a word of its own.

Jetlag is officially called "circadian desynchronization" or "desynchronosis." I call it Laggin' Dragon, in reference to that illusive beast who resides in the sky. When we travel through its realm, we become enshrouded in its cloak of discombobulation — a word which sounds a lot like the experience. Blurry, confused, lacking coordination, these words define discombobulation.

Here's another way to describe jetlag: it's like getting off a not-so-merry-go-round only to discover you're not even at an amusement park!

DRAGON'S DEN (Nature and Body Clocks)
Jetlag is definitely not psychological; it is cycle logical. The reason we experience jetlag is because all our internal cycles — such as temperature, sleep patterns, sexual desires, cravings for sweets, reactions to medications, susceptibility to illnesses, and more — are disrupted when we travel. Jetlag forces every instrument in our bodily orchestra, from salivation to elimination, to

change its tune. For a while, our fleshly symphony becomes a cacophony.

Whether we pay attention or not, all our bodily cycles wax and wane to cosmic rhythms. The most overt example of this, of course, is menstruation — the human female fertility cycle in synchronicity with the time it takes to go from one New Moon to the next.

Scientists have observed rhythms like this in the microscopic world of atoms and in the vast dimensions of stars. On Earth, too, all processes of life appear to fluctuate with predictable regularity.[6] This is as sure for all living things as the fact that the Sun rises every morning in the east and sets every evening in the west.

LAGGIN' DRAGON (Disruption of Body Clocks)

Yet, I've seen the Sun set many times in the east! When jetting west at over 620 mph, aircraft fly away from the eastern horizon faster than the rotation of the Earth, making the Sun appear to set in the east. It is a quirky kind of thing to see a sunrise set, to fly beyond the laws of Nature.

I've also seen, from windows of jets when flying west, numerous seemingly-eternal sunsets, as an evening Sun bobs up and down on the western horizon for hours. On one flight, this phenomenon of a rising sunset caused much consternation to a certain Jewish passenger who was attempting to salute the setting Sun (once and for all) with his traditional prayer. This man rose and sat, rose and sat, painfully unable to reconcile his ritual.

Disorientation is a well-known symptom of jetlag.

What takes place in our bodies on a cellular level is the reason for this disorientation, I believe. As our cycles uncouple from their old timezone, they also disengage from the healthy co-dependency which they maintain with each other. For example, body temperature is normally dependent upon our activity/sleep phases.[7]

Each uncoupled cycle (sleep, temperature, etc.) has its own clock and, thus, takes its own time to reset. So, after jetting, in addition to struggling towards the new zone, our cells are handicapped due to lack of team support. Additionally, the body tries to retain rhythmic stability,[8] which means that it resists change in a protective way. For example, in a normal, non-jetting lifestyle, this stability helps sustain us when missing a meal or a night's sleep.

Although appetite, sleep, and energy levels are usually restored to normal for the new timezone in a week or so, some hormonal adjustments can take as long as two months. Then, after they've been reset for the right time of day, they require even more time to achieve the amplitude which they had before leaving home.[9]

These time frames, of course, vary according to all extenuating circumstances of travel. These include the hour of departure/arrival, the direction/duration/altitude of flight, the season/altitude of embarkation/disembarkation, the aircraft type, the purpose of travel, the airline/class, the traveler's experience and health, and accumulated jetlag. All these variables are thoroughly explored in the following pages.

Body temperature is one way we can test ourselves for jetlag. How does yours differ when you travel? And how long does it takes for it to return to normal? For this, you need to establish your norm before leaving home, taking readings with a digital thermometer for at least a week, twice daily, in the mornings and evenings. For most people, temperature cyclically peaks around 5 p.m. and dips around 5 a.m.

When using an oral thermometer, avoid putting anything in your mouth ten minutes prior to a reading —

even toothpaste. Be aware, too, that infections, stress, ovulation, exercise, and pollution can also alter readings.

Temperature generally remains out of sync, doctors tell us, for a week after jetting.[10] The heart rate, too, takes about a week to beat the effects of jetlag. This fact supports my theory that it is exceedingly difficult to sustain *affairs of the heart* over long distances, wherein one party travels across multiple timezones to rendezvous with a beloved. Love, the act of merging oneself with another, requires a wholeness of being which cannot be attained when a heart is divided against itself by jetlag, or by any other state of disharmony.

People who suffer from cardiac weakness may have a less romantic concern about heartbeats. According to one cardiologist, "People with heart disease require longer to recover from any stress, including jetlag. They shouldn't fly at night or travel more than about three timezones without a rest stop."[11]

Jetlag modulates both the pulse and the yearnings of our hearts. It alters our brain waves; it stymies our capacity for comprehension. It affects our eyesight and insights, skews digestion and balance. It tampers with reproduction as well as creativity, with our sense of timing, and with the quality of our time.

DRAGON WATCH (The Globe and Its Timing)

If we residents of Earth have one common language at all, it is *time*. As we all adjust for the Earth's rotation from east to west, the clocks of those of us in the east are ahead of those of us in the west.

When we divide the Earth by twenty-four (the number of hours in a day), we're left with sections like those of an orange, narrow at the top and bottom and wider at the middle. On the fruit we call these segments; on the Earth we say they are timezones.

Jetting west across timezones slows down and lengthens the day. Conversely, jetting east shortens the day; here time appears to speed up and we are required to fast-forward our watches.

Just as we re-set the watches on our wrists, so we can expedite the re-setting our internal body clocks. JET SMART is a guide for how to do this. On the following pages the symbol ✈ highlights a specific cognitive choice to jet smart.

✈ When you first buckle up on board, set your watch to the local time at your arrival destination as a mental commitment to support the process of re-setting your biological cycles.

✈ Start regulating your sleep cycle en route; adjust inflight sleep to the aircraft's arrival time. For landing in the a.m., sleep as much as you can on board; for touchdowns in the p.m., don't sleep until after arrival.

✈ While en route, imagine you can actually see yourself after arrival, feeling safe, alert, healthy, content, and happy. This is a subtle and yet significantly effective way to reset biological cycles. Our cycles are programmable like computers. Program yours to bounce back from jetlag with adaptability and resilience by focusing your thoughts and feelings on the desired goal.

✈ After landing, schedule work or other important activity at a time when you are likely to have maximum energy. Most people are energized in the evenings after jetting east; after jetting west, we're generally our best in the mornings.

THE NATURE OF THE BEAST (Flying East or West)
The air above our Earth has currents, similar to those in the oceans. These jetstreams, or tunnels of air, are around 37,000 feet high. They move from west to east, as the world turns. For this reason, flying east is faster

and smoother than jetting west. For instance, eastbound from Los Angeles to London is several hours shorter than the return.

Ah, but flying west almost always produces less jetlag. (See WEIRD exceptions below.) In a series of studies, volunteers flew back and forth between six timezones to measure body temperature, fatigue, and cognitive-motor skills. Recovery was two to four days following westbound flights, but nine days after eastbound travel.[12]

This corresponds to my experience. We flight attendants used to be scheduled completely around the world, either east or west. The layovers were identical; nevertheless, the direction of travel made the two experiences entirely different. Westbound trips always went "senior." (Rank gets choice.)

✈ After jetting west, it's easier to adjust our sleep rhythms. For this reason, most westbound travelers experience less jetlag.

When flying west, we experience unnaturally long days. Fatigue prevails as the head hits the pillow. On the other hand (May I say wing?), adapting sleep eastbound, when the day/night ratio has been foreshortened, requires that we zonk out before we're really feeling tuckered out.

Take a simple case of jetlag between California and New York. If you habitually like to turn out your light at 10 p.m. in L.A., you will have to do so in New York at 7 p.m. (your bodyclock time). If you wait until you normally feel tired, you'll be dozing off at 1 a.m. (locally), which makes getting up at 6 a.m. a rather an uncomfortable expectation. (See CELESTIAL SLUMBER, page 35.)

There are two exceptions to the West-Easier-In-Resolving-Discombobulation (WEIRD) rule.

✈ After jetting east, sleep adjustments are generally easy for night owls, people who are most active at night.

✈ Coming home (no matter east or west) is easier than when you have to adjust your stance to a foreign dance, i.e., tune into the new local rhythms.

After a flight home, for example, many people have an increased sense of well-being — but not always. A number of frequent flyers have told me that they fight with their spouses after every trip. A closer investigation reveals that the everyday living situation of these couples is not aligned with their dreams and expectations. Jetlag limits their ability to tolerate frustration.

✈ When we are jetlagged, feelings become more apparent; it's as if the experience of jetlag leaves us transparent, exposing our emotional underpinnings.

A final quirky note sounds about jetting east or west when we cross the International Dateline. Here, in the middle of the Pacific Ocean, jetters gain or lose a whole day. On eastbound legs, there is the peculiar illusion of living the same day twice. Westbound, passengers miss a day altogether. Though it's only an illusion, this calendar mix-up usually takes on a particular human significance — especially when it comes to birthdays and Christmas!

DRAGON LOADSTONE (Magnetic Fields)
Flying east or west, according to scientists, is the only way to get jetlag. Flying north or south, they all agree, results in no jetlag.

With all respect, the results of my research (a few thousand fights east/west and a couple hundred roundtrips north/south) reveals the following: flying east/west upsets the sleep cycle. This is tiring. In contrast, flying north/south upsets our water balance. Since water is over 90% of the liquid content of our blood, this shift dilutes our ability to function in numerous ways.

Consider the flow cycle of water. Down Under, everything goes down the drain in a counter-clockwise direction, just the opposite of the way it flows in the Northern Hemisphere. If these forces have such dramatic effect on water in a sink, how could they not affect the water within the reservoirs of the human body? (Is not the bladder a "sink" of urine?)

Water gets agitated in transitions. If you sit in a bathtub and create a wave action, then suddenly change your rhythm, for a while the water is choppy before it settles into its new flow. In the same way, travelers feel an extra lag going Down Under — a jetlag lag.

East/west jetlag is generally at its worst ebb within twenty-four hours after travel; north/south hemispheric displacement hits its low later commencing on the second to third day after arrival. The latter is a two-step process: before our cells can adopt the new pervasive rhythms, their molecular structure needs to realign with the new polarity.

Fluids, like crystals, orient towards the closest, strongest magnetic influence — in particular, the North and South Poles. When we displace ourselves hemispherically (by jet travel) from a familiar magnetic field to a surrogate one, we feel as though we have become unplugged.

One of four spark plugs in my car jarred loose last week, though I didn't know it at first. What I noticed was that I had difficulty starting the car and climbing the steep driveway from my cottage. After a couple of days I went to a service station; the mechanic looked under the hood, found the loose connection, and restored all power with a simple nudge to one of the wires.

The point is, even a small electrical disruption can result in a serious loss of power. To restore all power after long-distance equator vaulting, our internal compasses need to be reset just as ships' compasses do after they shift hemispheres. Ships constructed in the Northern Hemisphere and operating in the Southern require constant realignments with small magnets; adjustments can take up to twenty years![13]

Scientists have noted how shifts in geo-magnetic fields can cause in us a lack of motor coordination resulting in increased accidents.[14]

✈ After landing, to expedite magnetic-field adjustment, sleep in a bed aligned with the Earth's north/south axis, with the crown of your head towards the North Pole.

Occasionally, I prefer to sleep with my head towards the South. If you wish to tune into this subtle energy, try lying both ways on your bed and see if you can feel the difference. One direction has a stronger beat, like a gentle pulsing entering the crown of the head and palpitating out the center of the feet.

The Earth's magnetism also affects us emotionally, influencing what we're attracted to and what we attract to us. Out-of-sync magnetic fields can be experienced as loss of gut feeling and erratic behavior.

✈ When traveling between hemispheres, consider a near-equator rest stop. Here, magnetic fields are less intense, and so we are less affected by them.

Flying north/south also plunges travelers into a total seasonal disruption. It can be disorienting, though entertaining, to go from spring to fall in a matter of hours. I always get the sensation that a camcorder has been superimposed over my eyes, and the cinematographer, outside myself, is an amateur playing with the zoom. In and out I go, too fast, as I fly to and fro Down Under.

THE DRAGON'S TALE (Travel Experience)
When we're familiar with the ins and outs of a route, city, hotel, airports, and so on, we experience less jetlag.

Always remember, the dragon you know is less intimidating than the dragon you don't.

✈ When we've traveled to a foreign environment before, are familiar with its noises, smells, and essence, we feel an innate sense of security — translating into less jetlag.

✈ If you haven't made a trip before, it's best to review the journey in detail with someone who has. Or, study up.

Fortunately, travel experiences are easily retained. I've noticed that whatever I experience in a locale, I never seem to lose; it appears to wait for me there, in something like a thought-form which looks like a clone of myself. Still today, these clones are stationed around the world like favorite seasonal outfits stored in some colossal cosmic closet, ready for me to step into as I re-enter those zones.

We all experience this; maybe this is why we keep wanting to find new places to visit, with new vibrations, to invigorate untapped aspects of ourselves.

On the down side of travel experience, people who mega-jet for years without stopping to rest come down with what I call *mega-lag*. An example of mega-lag is the story of Lowell Thomas, the radio commentator, who was hospitalized in the sixties for a heart attack; later, he publicly stated that his illness was chronic jetlag.[15]

To know if you might have mega-lag, consider if you're eligible for any of the airlines' frequent flyer bonus awards. For instance, if you've flown 20,000 miles, you get a free economy roundtrip ticket on some airlines. One can accumulate 20,000 miles with a mere four roundtrips from New York to the West Coast. The more bonus awards you accumulate, the more mega-lag you accumulate.

Years of mega-lag can be likened to years of alcohol consumption. One does gain dexterity and coping strategies; however, it's not possible to develop immunity. In fact, like alcoholics, *jetlaggards* do develop ways to look good outwardly while running the risk of deteriorating mind and organs in the long run. Like alcoholism, the high-altitude environment inhibits oxidation and is addictive.[16]

People who fly for a living are generally up in the air too much to find out if it's addictive — they don't stop long enough to notice the craving and other withdrawal symptoms.

Flight attendants officially take off their gold wings at age 65. Pilots must retire at age 60; engineers (the third person in a three man cockpit) may work till 65. Some captains retire, then fly in an engineer's seat for five more years. While active, crew accumulate about a half a million miles/year.

For short-term jetlag, there's an old rule of thumb: roughly one day of rest to recover for every timezone crossed. For mega-lag, there are no rules. No scientific studies have been done, to date, on the health and longevity of those who mega-jet.

Nevertheless, I did notice, at the end of a report from the British Air Line Pilots Association, that 60% of pilot premature retirement is due to cardiovascular disease.[17] In addition, a "study of Canadian pilots showed an increased risk of brain cancer."[18]

My own research reveals mega-lag symptoms of chronic fatigue, swollen lymph glands, weak kidneys, hyperactive adrenal glands, eye sensitivity, headache, muscle twitching, temporary amnesia, susceptibility to staph infection, and the recurrent, addictive urge to jetaway.

Tony O'Reilly, the high-society, jetsetting CEO (Heinz, Weightwatchers, Waterford), commented on his life-style of frenetic commutes across the Atlantic with the poignant one-liner: "It is a formula for an early grave."[19]

Today, many other business execs prefer video teleconferencing to continent hopping. Even Boeing, the aircraft manufacturer, boasts to have saved five million miles, so far, with video-linkups for their executives.[20]

In conclusion, MEETING THE DRAGON has elucidated some of the basic challenges we jetters face. The next section, FACING THE DRAGON, offers hope. Learn how to choose a flightplan which will upgrade you to Smart Class. We chart our course with the courage to remain alert. We take off with a willingness to provide ourselves with all necessary remedies. In addition, we remember to focus on well-being, moment by moment, to insure a safe, comfortable touchdown.

Facing the Dragon

ALL TOGETHER NOW

TURN THE YOKE (Jetlag Remedies)

During my years of service as an international flight attendant, many remedies have crossed my flight path. A man once told me with all sincerity that you have to buy a whiskey miniature on board and then drink it all down the minute your foot hits the new land; he believed booze shocks the system into rejecting all foreign bacteria. Another passenger encouraged me to "wear brown paper grocery bags" inside my shoes.

Then, there are those who practice the proverbial ostrich technique, pretending that the best cure for jetlag is to act like it doesn't exist! And there's the oblivious-to-the-world technique — at-numb-ness — either get plastered on alcohol, zonked on pills, buzzed on sugar, whatever.

After some experimentation I opted for holistic remedies. "Symptoms," of course, are *bodily signals*. When we listen to them and make adjustments, inner harmony revives along with outward well-being. In other words, watch the indicators on your instrument panel. If you're flying off course, turn the yoke (cockpit steering wheel), and resume your optimum flight plan.

After jetting, our internal clocks naturally reset themselves in their own time, according to our limitations of age, resilience, and disposition, as well as those imposed by all present extenuating circumstances — everything from motion sickness to marital problems. However, to expedite jetlag clearance, there are specific actions we can take.

Some travelers are obliged to take more action than others. Imagine, if you will, that you are just out of high school, in excellent health. Then, suppose you neglect yourself for a few years, you drink in excess, and you forget to exercise. Your health will, most likely, maintain itself for a while. However, if you neglect yourself for fifteen years, or more, it's quite probable you'll feel it — possibly lethargy, maybe low back pain, or headaches.

Similarly, if you neglect to care for yourself on a five-hour flight and you fly only now and again, you may not feel it. However, for frequent flyers with mileage awards of mega-lag, our normal routine just isn't enough to help us stay healthy, alert, and at our best while flying — we have to work at it.

The object of this book is to enable passengers to become aware of imbalances triggered by jet travel and then to give people the wherewithal to select from the suggested remedies, as needed. In the previous chapter, symptoms of jetlag were divided into the four headings — physical, mental, emotional, and spiritual — for the purposes of classification and understanding. Remedies, however, cannot be so classified because integration is inherent in the cure. For example, when we address our bodies' nutritional needs, we automatically provide ourselves with wholesome food for thought.

PIE IN THE SKY (Travel Diet)

For many passengers, airline meals are the anticipated highlight, then the disappointing *lowlight* of flights. People often ask me what's the best thing to eat on jets. Vegetarian since the sixties, I confess to purist tendencies — and from this level of emancipation I avoid all constipation (usually).

There isn't really anything I would recommend eating on commercial jets except, maybe, the bread out of Frankfurt. However, I haven't flown first class on Singapore Airlines; I've heard they're the best. The airline services I've seen are typically high in fat, full of sugar and salt, chemically processed, bland, with pasty sauces, and lacking wholesome complex carbohydrates.

And, after all, airline meals are only frozen dinners, not fresh food. They are heated in aluminum pans, not glass or copper pots. Gas or even electric burners are not available, only convection ovens. Flight attendants are not trained chefs; moreover, since deregulation (1978), attendants are regularly handicapped by malfunctioning ovens and carts. (See THE BUDGET MONSTER, page 73.)

I've wondered how, in particular, first-class passengers can pack away an eleven-course meal in flight with their organs already swollen from low air pressure! (See DROWNING IN MID AIR, page 53.) The choice, of course, is an individual one: arrive energetic, or drag heavy guts of undigested excess baggage, then spend a week struggling with the body's demands for meals at odd hours.

I can understand how airline meal services create a false sense of marking time. Yet, the meal is not served on local time of either departure or arrival city.

I've seen how "the service" even tempts people who aren't hungry! *Plane* boredom?

Some flyers prefer "special meals." The airlines will

cater to low-cholesterol, kosher, vegetarian, Hindu (spicy vegetarian), Moslem (no pork), children's, and fruit-only diets.

✈ Of all the special meals on jets, the fruit plate is usually the most fresh and gets my seal of approval.

Unfortunately, even though a special meal is ordered in advance, it is often not delivered to the flight.

✈ To insure that you get your special meal follow these three steps:

Step One: Ask the name of the person who takes your order as well as the *record locater number*.

Step Two: When you check in, ask if your meal request is *in the computer*.

Step Three: When you board, ask the galley attendant if it's *been loaded*. Then, to expedite timely delivery, hand her a paper with your name, seat number, and meal preference.

From a nutritional viewpoint, bouncing back from jetlag requires daily proper eating habits. However, some people claim that just a couple days of diet change will do the trick. The Argonne anti-jet-lag diet touts this, recommending alternating meals of high protein with those of high carbohydrate.[21]

The Argonne diet presumes that high-carbohydrate meals make us sleep. This has been my experience, too, but only when I eat extra-large portions. Otherwise, I can sustain energy over long periods, like a horse — and as a flight attendant I've worked like one!

Further, among mountain climbers it is known that a pure carbohydrate diet gives one an "altitude advantage" of about 2,000 feet; i.e., climbers have found that they can function on less oxygen on a pure carbohydrates diet.[22] This altitude advantage is extremely helpful to jet travelers, too. (See DROWNING IN MID AIR, page 53.) So it makes no sense to eat any high protein meals, Argonne-style, when jetting.

I feel it is also important to note that the Argonne diet was developed in a lab by studying rats that never crossed a single timezone — so I was told by a researcher when I called there. "Can the effects of time-zone shifts be realistically simulated in laboratory experiments?"[23] queries another group of scientists. A further study on the Argonne diet justifies this skepticism, finding that "The subjects NOT on the diet fared better than those on it."[24]

Since 1983, when the diet was first published, people have been trying to make some sense of it. For this reason, I feel I need to say one more thing about it. The diet recommends fasting on travel days, and, by definition, I agree. However, they've misconstrued the concept "fast." On Argonne fast days, passengers can consume eggs, low-fat cheese, skim milk, butter, tuna, salmon, chicken, vegetables, juices, bread, mayonnaise, any kind of salad dressing, and alcohol.

Fast, according to the dictionary, is "to eat very little or nothing."

✦ When jetting, adjust your digestive system by fasting (no solid food) the whole time you are in transit.

✦ If it is not appropriate for you to fast, pack some carbohydrate snacks. Grains, such as shredded wheat or crackers, are excellent totes. Leftovers from your favorite restaurant are always delicious at 40,000 feet. Or, consider bringing a raw potato to cook on board. You'll have to wait until the regular meal service is over, then ask a galley attendant to throw it in an empty oven, 450° for one hour.

✦ When snacking, consider taking vitamins — a multiple with minerals (one with every repast) and a vitamin C (buffered, time-released, 1000-6000 mg per twenty-four hours). While fasting, however, I find it best to skip vitamins.

✈ Hour of departure, duration of flight, restrictions of agriculture, room in your carry-on, as well as the advice of your physician, all need to be taken into consideration when deciding whether to fast or snack en route.

✈ Don't eat just because your wristwatch says it's time, or just because a service has commenced. In fact, on travel days, with connecting flights, it's quite common to be served five meals during a normal three-meal time-frame.

✈ After fasting in the air, break fast gently with a light meal on the ground.

✈ Suppose we all stopped eating on jets. Not only would jetlag be reduced, but also (maybe) fares, to boot! (In the first quarter of 1991, American Airlines alone spent $125 million on food.)[25]

Eating is idiosyncratic. It serves many functions. It's a form of energy. It's social. It reminds us of our childhood. It's a substitute for sex. This is why I suggest that you do your own "food thing" when traveling — as long as you use your best-informed judgment while continuing to tune into your own bodily signals.

MILEAGE MARATHON (Exercise)
As far as physical activity goes, jet travel is like a sandwich. On the outside are spurts of aerobic activity at odd hours before and after flights. In the center is the spread of static conformity in seats confining and tight.

As travelers we often perform unaccustomed tasks, from grueling trips in public transports, to long treks in terminals *schlepping* carry-ons for what seems like miles. Once on board, we rush and contort to stow our carry-ons. Disembarking, also rushing, we retrieve them, then drag them downstairs (when there's no jetway), and lug them on and off customs counters and in and out of ground vehicles.

✈ Like an athlete, train yourself for the airport trek. Close your suitcases a few days before departure, and try them around the house for size and weight, even lift the carry-on as you would into one of those storage bins above the seats, about six feet high.

✈ Do not over-pack; heavy luggage can be fatiguing and expensive. Stay within the airline's limits for weight and dimensions. These vary, so check ahead.

Although the space on jets is extremely limited, numerous exercises are possible on flights. After some hours in the air, passengers often feel like zoo animals in too-small cages — fed, dull, but agitated. The longer the flighttime, indeed, the greater the need for activity.

The next few pages detail suggested moves for passengers on commercial jets. Of course, it's smart to consult your own physician before starting new exercises. Then, progress at your own pace. Perhaps do a few, then cross a timezone or two. Do a few more, then stop to snack. Or, take a nap.

✈ **The Sky's The Limit.** While in your seat, slowly contract, then release, every muscle you can think of. Tense, then relax, isolating in succession: your feet, your legs, your perineum, your stomach, your chest, your arms, your neck, your face, your crown.

✈ **Let Your Body Lead The Way.** You may find, in an hour or so, that you suddenly have an urge to raise your knees, alternating right/left, to a count of ten.

Or, that you want to lean over into a forward bend, then, just hang out.

Or, that your wrists and ankles decide it's time to turn

like pinwheels.

Or, that your arms feel like reaching for the sky (inhale, exhale) for the benefit of your lungs.

✈ Count Your Blessings. If you're a less-strenuous type you might focus on relaxing your sphincter muscle, while at the same time forgiving yourself and others for anything and everything.

For what? You know best.

✈ Then, imagine a great weight lifted off your spine. *See* fresh red corpuscles emerge from each vertebra to join their brothers and sisters in your bloodstream. This new blood will nourish you in the jetstream.

✈ Get Up And Circuit The Plane. When attendants are not involved in a major service, blocking the aisles with their carts, be smart — get out of your seat and promenade, ramble, march.

✈ Or, walk like Groucho with straight back and slightly bent knees. This pumps even more blood up to the brain. Not only that, the Groucho walk is easy on the knees, as the jet's thin metal flooring has a trampoline effect. Also notice the floor's angle; most jets today fly nose up to save on fuel.

✈ While circuiting your jet, feel free to peruse galley centers. Here, find hot-water spigots for making your own herb tea, or instant soup, whenever you want. Ask a flight attendant to brief you on spigot etiquette when she's not busy.

Other highlights on your tour may include: magazines (usually stowed in the side or back bulkhead partitions); inflight electronics (some jets project maps with altitude readings, flight path, time, date, and gate); and telephones, (they only work over land with land-based cell-sites).

You may also want to take note of the no-smoking zones and clusters of lavs. Also, keep a lookout for fire extinguishers and portable oxygen bottles, placarded with very small labels either up on overhead compartments or down on small bustle compartments behind the last row of seats of each section.

In any event, it's fun just to check out a $150 million vehicle.

✈ **The Squat.** Squat down with feet flat and forearms (or elbows, or armpits) resting on knees. Remain in squat as long as you are comfortable. Try to extend your time. Lean forward, rock to and fro, or circle around. Then, when returning to standing, use the inner-leg muscles to rise so that you avoid straining the knees.

The squat elasticizes the largest muscles in the body, the hamstrings, which run from the back of the knees to the buttocks. To "hamstring" someone means to disable them. Don't allow your body to be hamstrung from sitting immobile for hours in jets. Take time out to squat by an exit, or in a lav. (Be considerate when there's a line.) First-class passengers have room by their seats.

✈ For those travelers without a regular stretching practice, such as yoga or martial arts, the squat is especially important. Stretching accelerates acclimatization. Flexible bodies coexist with resilient emotions, breaking the grip of the irrascibility so characteristic of jetlag.

✈ To be most effective as a jetlag remedy, stretching should be done on board, as well as right before sleep.

✈**Metaphysical Athletics**. Close your eyes and travel to a place in your mind where the air is crystal clear. Take all the time you need to *enthuse* a peak experience. For instance, see yourself walking (inhale) on an autumn morning, striding (exhale) along a winding, sun-dappled pathway. Sunlight gleams through a montage of colorful leaves on trees. Hear the leaves crackling underfoot.

You prefer jogging? Sprint (inhale, exhale) along a wide sandy beach. Hear ocean waves crash as they lap at your feet (inhale, exhale).

Dive into the pale green water. It is warm and silky. Iridescent sparkles dazzle each little crest. Swim out from the shore (inhale, exhale). Stretch with confident, powerful strokes. Hear little splashes as your hands cut the water.

You have a preference for frozen water? Go skiing. It's that perfect powder morning. The air is crisp blue-white. Snow flies by your face as you bob and weave effortlessly.

✈ Float freely to pleasant places in your mind's eye. Remain internally light, not too serious, like the wafer-thin cirrus clouds outside, matching feelings to the awesomeness of higher altitudes. Then, with any incoming breath, open your eyes and smile.

✈ **Practice Telepathy.** In perfect detail in your mind, create the picture of a message you want to send someone on Earth. See it in vivid color; hear it spoken. Then condense it into a little ball of light, and *zap* it on its way. See it received and acknowledged.

After arrival, ask the person to whom you transmitted, "Hey, what happened at such and such time?" Maybe s/he thought of you then, made plans for your visit, fixed up the guest room. Check it out. Some day we might discover that telepathy works best from jets, where we can operate like satellites.

✈ **Aerobics After Landing.** Tennis, a swim, a jog, dancing, weight lifting — go for whatever is available and what you enjoy most.

✈ Jetlaggards who crave *collapsation* or hibernation should really resist the temptation. Walk with coordination. Breathe with intoxication. Be your own inspiration. Mutter a magic incantation. This is the way to quick regeneration.

✈ For those travelers without a regular magic incantation practice, may I suggest: *All the living cells of my body work in perfect harmony. I am well, and how, and clearly present in the here and now.*

✈ Walking in the realm of Nature is an antidote for any brand of jetlag. City parks, botanical gardens, and zoos are places to roam when we're away from home, helping travelers revive and acclimatize.

Long walks after landing satisfy the legs' need to move, the mind's need to be entertained, and the cells' propensity to soak up local light and color.

BIKINIS & FURS (Meteorological Virtues)
Many scientists now recommend doses of light (natural and/or artificial) to help jetters and some of these recommendations actually conflict with each other. One scientist tells us to go outdoors at the new locale when it's sunrise-time back home. For instance, after flying from New York to Paris, across six timezones, be outside in the "city of light" around 2 p.m.[26] Another researcher recommends precisely-timed three-hour bright lights for three days after travel to reset the body's clocks; he warns us that incorrect light exposures will deepen jetlag and, in particular, we must avoid morning light, whether flying east or west.[27] However, the medical director of the United Nations extols morning light after flying east to speed up metabolism and afternoon rays after flying west to slow it down.[28]

Prescribing therapeutic light for jetlag evidently

involves more than meets the eye. Nevertheless, farm-
ers have used light for centuries to modify metabolism.
Songbirds are made to sing in winter when they are normally silent, and hens are made to lay more eggs. All it
takes is light.

However, hens sometimes peck each other to death
in crowded conditions under bright lights;[29] and humans
suffer ill effects, too, from unseasonably extended or
diminished periods of light: irritability, restlessness,
recklessness, and sleeping difficulties.

When contemplating a formula for therapeutic light
in conjunction with jetlag, we need to factor in departure and arrival times and latitudes, along with the sum
total of transit hours under fluorescents at airports and
on jets, as well as glare reflected off glaciers on polar
routes, and, on westbound long-hauls (nonstops over
ten hours), bright daylight streaming in aircraft windows for hours. For example, the long-haul from New
York to Tokyo departs around noon and lands fourteen
hours later — the whole time in bright daylight without
a tint of twilight, night, or dawn.

On top of this, daylight above the clouds is clearer and
more brilliant than the sunlight which is filtered down to
us on land, and this also has a more energizing effect on
us. Thus, the duration and intensity of light exposures we
travelers are flooded with en route can make any desire
to go in search of extra light after landing, as scientists
are now suggesting, about as appealing as subjecting oneself to a searing spotlight of interrogation.

None of these many considerations, however, denies
the basic principle: as a therapeutic aid for jetlag, natural light is quite effective.

✈ Tune in to light as it fluctuates in your immediate
environment, from moment to moment, when traveling. Give yourself light (natural, whenever possible)

according to your own energy requirements. For example, if you are tired and need to stay awake, sunlight or bright indoor lights can quicken the pulse. For relaxation or sleep, candlelight or filtered daylight through curtains or blinds is fine.

In relation to skirting the planet, there are two more aspects to light management which I have observed.

✦ When flying east in winter from a near-Equator locale (for example, Hawaii) to a higher-latitude location (such as New York), the shorter day-to-night ratio helps to slow down metabolism.

✦ When flying west from higher latitudes to a near-Equator locale, tropical skies can help speed up our metabolism.

How to take advantage of these speed-ups and slow-downs? This happens automatically when we are outdoors. Even being in a room with windows during daylight periods enlightens our body clocks; the larger the windows the stronger the entrainment. The important thing is this: after jetting, don't hole up inside all day, away from natural light.

✦ Being outdoors in natural light as much as possible for at least three days after flying automatically cues our cells to the local cosmology.

Some scientists maintain that human beings can only input environmental light through the eyes. They claim, in this sense, we are less adaptable than birds or lizards which perceive light in other ways. It is this writer's judgment, however, that these scientists are wearing blinders. Many times I have *felt* the Sun rise before seeing it.

For example, during the decades when I was pirouetting around the planet, I became a fan of sunrises and sunsets from the spectacular vantage points of jet windows. I was surprised myself when my inner clock started cuing me for these events. Even in the middle of a busy service, without a moment to spare, I'd get that certain feeling to glance out a porthole, just in sync with a sunrise. And, on layovers, too, even behind an eye-mask and blackout curtains, regardless of what timezone I was on, or how much sleep I'd missed, I'd often wake up, uncannily alert, in tune with the Sun's transition.

I've witnessed countless phenomenal heavenly light shows around the globe — complete with green flashes, those emerald light bursts a second before/after a sunrise/sunset.

We all have this metaphysical gift within reach. Haven't you ever set yourself a wakeup call without an alarm clock?

One does not need penetrating insight to prepare for climate change, another facet of jet-related meteorological character which impacts travelers. Temperature differentials between departure and arrival locales can shock the system of even the most seasoned flyer.

For example, every winter, residents from Hawaii (humid hot) rush to Colorado (dry cold) to ski; and movie moguls migrate back and forth between Palm Springs (dry hot) and London (humid cold).

✈ My coping strategy for the radical shift from hot climates to cold entails confronting the first bite of cold air head on, with these three steps:

Step One. Brace with vitamin B_3 (niacin). After touchdown I take 100 milligrams of natural niacin. Soon I am feeling very warm all over — a tingling, almost itching sensation which persists usually long enough to make the transition out of an airport and into a hotel.

Step Two. Use deep-heating lotion (sold over-the-counter) rubbed on chest, kidney area, and feet.

Step Three. Don an under-layer of silk longjohns. Silk is conveniently wearable and transportable.

One North Dakota airport has a novel solution for its ill-prepared winter travelers: police pull scantily-clad disembarking passengers aside to offer them overcoats on loan. If you're using my ultra-light formula (niacin, deep-heating lotion, and longjohns) in Bismarck, be forewarned. Anyway, let's tip our berets to North Dakota, for leading the way towards noble global warming!

Each world locale has its unique micro-climate: humidity, temperature, altitude, wind, barometric pressure, and ion count, all simmered with natural geology and man-made technology into a one-of-a-kind recipe. ✈ After landing, as you step outside the terminal, take time to feel your senses shift between your former world and your new environment. Give your cells the maximum opportunity to begin acclimatization. Don't rush them from vehicle to vehicle, plane to train. Don't railroad your senses! This is the time for sampling and discerning, with heightened awareness, the new meteorological virtues.

CELESTIAL SLUMBER (Sleep at Night)

Jetlag researchers have found that along with "climate cues," "food triggers" (adoption of local meal times and foods) and "social interaction ticklers" (doing what the locals do) also help us to adapt in new timezones.

When in Rome do as the Romans do. This is not an attempt to inflame anyone's appetite for spaghetti, spumoni, or sex — just a reminder to operate on local time. For example, it's always beneficial to sleep when it's night locally — healthfully, fiscally, and socially. Accordingly, adjust your bedtime to the local timetable as soon as possible after landing. Otherwise, pay the price of nighttime insomnia and/or daytime inertia: tourists gripe that they "space out" the best sites; businessmen snore through meetings.

Sleeping at night is something most of us take for granted at home, where we function on automatic pilot. After jetting, however, we need to take responsibility for re-setting our sleep cycles.

✈ Sleep at night wherever you may be, and you'll bounce back from jetlag expeditiously.

While adjustment of our sleep cycle to the new local clock ameliorates most of the so-called "inappropriate sleepiness" associated with jetlag, it does not necessarily stop those bubbles of drowsiness which may surface on the third or fourth day as the second wave of jetlag catches up with us. However, this second wave of jetlag is only a small swell to quell, if we've had the will to adopt the new, nightly rhythms.

Sometimes, especially after a nightflight with an a.m. arrival, going straight to bed is what we crave most. Resist if you can, as this will, generally, inhibit recovery. The reason? First, we are usually not tired enough to sleep again that night. Second, entrainment of the sleep cycle takes place when we're asleep; if we do this the first morning, we're actually notifying our cells that we want them to ascribe to a morning sleep cycle.

"When I fly from the U.S. to Europe, I stay up all day and go to bed at the usual local time," confirms tennis pro Stefan Edberg.[30]

An opposing jetlag theory is this: stay on home time while abroad. However, positive results are only reaped from this approach on short trips — for instance, turnarounds of less than forty-eight hours, or when crossing only one or two timezones. Otherwise, staying on home-time also inhibits recovery. At new locales our cells act befuddled: they hear the old zone sing her haunting melody while, simultaneously, they lend an ear to the new songs and hanker to learn the local dances.

A third approach to jetlag is to gradually adapt your bedtime to the new zone before leaving home. However, I just can't agree. Isn't it enough that we have to make traumatic sleep adjustments every time we travel? Why inflict them prematurely upon ourselves? After long-distance flights we must face the music anyway. Deal with the shift naturally, in the moment.

After landing in a new zone, the Almighty Law Of Timezones (A LOT) automatically assists us. Always remember, those who dare to prematurely violate A LOT go against the force. The wrath of self-imposed sleeplessness is the penalty of such folly. Go when the force is with you.

Some people have such a hard time regulating their sleep that they resort to sleeping pills. Sleepers can be divided into two clearly polarized camps regarding the use of prescription medication for transient insomnia associated with jetlag — those who swear by sleeping pills, and those who wouldn't touch them with a ten-foot barge pole from Bangkok.

Proponents claim flying is easy when you can just zonk out on departure and doze away flight tedium. Even President Bush used them for long flights;[31] that was until reporters started suggesting that some of his strange speech patterns such as referring to the Nitty Gritty Dirt Band as the "Nitty Ditty Nitty Gritty Great Bird"[32] may have been caused by sleeping pills. On another continent, Boris Yeltsin's aids have now publically stated that their boss' slurred speech in the U.S. was not due to drinking bouts, but "sleeping pills he had taken to combat jet lag."[33]

If these heads of state are having trouble handling

sleeping pills when they travel, what about us normal folk without a staff to watch over us? How do we manage, for example, if there is an emergency on board, and we're under the pall of sleeping pills?

One flight attendant who worked the 737 which ripped open at 24,000 feet (4/88), exposing eighty-nine terrified passengers to the wild blue yonder, recalled: "I was collecting empty glasses when, suddenly, a thunderous blast knocked me out of my shoes. A passenger helped hold me to the floor, so I would not be thrown around."[34]

Presumably this passenger hadn't taken sleeping pills!

Even without such close encounters, sleeping pills, when used in conjunction with jetlag, are known to have a bizarre side-effect — short-term memory loss.[35] In addition, thirty deaths, to date, have been attributed to withdrawal symptoms.[36] Of course, each passenger will deal with jetlag as he or she chooses. I, categorically, will not endorse the use of sleeping pills as a travel aid.

Some jetlag scientists rave about synthetic melatonin to simulate a brain chemical which, they say, accounts for sleepiness at night. As usual, though, the announcement of this synthetic wonder has been followed by warnings of side-effects. For example, "melatonin is a possible inhibitor of sexual development in rats."[37]

The truth is, we're all starting to realize that we can't trick our bodies with anesthetizing chemicals forever; somewhere adjustments will be made. Holistic doctors are adamant that pharmaceuticals only postpone, and sometimes even hamper, this inescapable process of balancing out.

Finally, it's best to be awake for every flight descent, in order to consciously adjust your ears. Sleeping pills impede this process. (See NO POP, page 104.)

Eileen Ford, the duenna of the prestigious Ford Model Agency, travels first class around the world several times each year in search of more "perfect" faces, like those of her other million-dollar dolls: Christie Brinkley, Lauren Hutton, and Cheryl Tiegs. When Ms. Ford stated with perfect frankness, "You could hit me over the head with a hammer and I still wouldn't sleep on a plane,"[38] she encapsulated the sentiments of many night flyers.

On the other wing, when Marlon Brando was my passenger on a nightflight in the late sixties between Los Angeles and Papeete, he managed to sleep all flight through — as though he had been knocked on the head with a hammer!

After dinner, Mr. Brando pulled out the center armrest between his first-class seat and that of his son, and fixed a bed for his boy. Then, the star fell asleep on the floor, between his pair of seats and the ones in front of them.

He slept soundly until breakfast, his legs stretched across the aisle of our 707 (a narrow-body aircraft with only one aisle). I couldn't bring myself to wake him, to tell him his Levi-clad landing gear were violating an FAA Regulation by impeding access to exits. So, instead, all night I quietly stepped back and forth over him, each time wondering if Marlon Brando would glance up.

Often, on long-hauls when the economy section is sparsely populated, first-class passengers wander back to sleep. Their high-priced seats, even fully reclined with footrests extended, don't allow the center of the body to get horizontal. I've found that posture (when I've flown up front on vacations) actually cramps my ability to drop into the kind of deep sleep I am able to access when I'm lucky enough to score a whole row of seats in the back. I suspect this is because hormone rhythms are posture-dependent.[39]

In the early eighties, JAL offered sleeping berths for a

20% surcharge on the first class fare (about $200 on the Los Angeles/Tokyo sector). That's how much people want to lie down on planes! Airbus will soon introduce sleeping quarters on the A340 to twenty wealthy passengers. The compartments are to be located below deck in the cargo hold; it will be interesting to see what the emergency escape procedures are for these lucky few — as well as everything else that goes on down there!

Ideally, we would always travel during the day, then fall into restorative slumber at the nighttime of our destination. Red-eye specials, however, are about 20% cheaper than regular daytime fares. And, the night traveler also saves the price of a hotel room, so the thriftiness of red-eyes can be alluring.

There is really no substitute for eight contiguous hours in a bed. But, for those passengers who are interested in my technique on how to sleep in an airplane seat, turn to HOW TO SLEEP ON JETS, page 127.

Many passengers also have trouble falling asleep after arrival, particularly after eastbound flights, when night appears to arrive too soon. As a crewmember, I became an adept at falling asleep whenever wherever.

✈ My routine for sleep after eastbound flights entails these four steps:

Step One: I eat my main meal of the day.

Step Two: I take a long, hot bath in semi-darkness. I light a candle (some hotels provide them), or keep the door ajar using only a little light from the next room.

Step Three: I darken my bedroom as much as possible with curtains or blinds. I close off all windows of the body, with eye-mask and ear plugs. I lie down comfortably under the covers and pull them up over my mouth.

Step Four: I imagine I am outside my body. I see my body asleep, as if from the other side of the room. Then,

I trick myself as follows: I send my awareness into the sleeping form. As my imagination merges with my perception, I am asleep.

Sleep deprivation can touch our well-being on every level, even where we may notice it least — emotionally. MIT researchers reported that even though their subjects claimed to be unaffected, symptoms became apparent, in particular, irritability, beginning twenty-four hours after the period of missed sleep.[40]

✈ Sleep deprivation, along with the many other stressors of jetlag, can easily expose our raw emotions, such as irritability. Consciously balance yours, in whatever way works best for you (writing, talking to someone, screaming when you're alone in a safe place, etc.).

✈ For balancing my emotions while flying, I've found the following combination of flower essences (available at healthfood stores) an excellent travel aid. I mix a few drops of each essence in my own bottle of water, and regularly sip from it en route.

> *Rescue*, to soften the effects of stress in general,
> *Walnut*, to add stability during transition periods,
> *Scleranthus*, to stabilize mood swings, and
> *Yarrow*, to strengthen the subtle body.

AH, THERE'S THE RUB (Bodywork)

According to popular opinion, flight attendants have a "special friend" at every port. As soon as possible after every landing (so goes the myth) we escape into his/her arms for instant bodywork!

Who am I to burst this colorful, collective bubble of fantasy? I will tell you, however, that I've availed myself of bodywork all over the world — traditional forms such as Swedish massage, Japanese Shiatsu, Chinese acupuncture, and also non-traditional modalities including polarity, reflexology, acupressure, cranial-sacral — and, yes, *once in a while along the way, love has been good to me.*

One night George Harrison, the former Beatle, was in first class out of Sydney; his traveling companion, a Chinese acupuncturist. When all the other passengers were asleep, George kept me company with his bright eyes and stimulating conversation. There was another passenger who kept *shushing* us. "Shush, shush," she chastened the star. Finally the woman hissed, "Keep quiet, you two, I want to sleep!" George said, "She needs acupuncture," then quietly returned to his seat.

It's great to have bodyworkers in your circle of friends. Though most of us tend to think of bodywork as a luxury, it is, in fact, a preventative way to stay healthy. Our bodies have invisible rivers in which energy flows through us. The Chinese call this "chi," the Hawaiians "mana," the Hindus "prana" and "life force." When the current flows unimpeded, all flourishes on the banks (our organs). If there are dams (areas of tension), floods result above (flu), or it becomes parched below (constipation).

✈ Energy blocks (caused by tension/toxins/jetlag) are released through bodywork, along with endorphins.

✈ Choosing a bodyworker is like choosing a partner: Do you trust this person? Are you able to communicate?

Bodywork is also something you can do on yourself. A facial or foot massage actually stimulates all the organs.

✈ In flight, massage your feet and calves. Find places of tension (hard tight places which hurt) and take deep breaths while you work them.

✈ As an alternative routine, try skin brushing after flight. In France they sell *friction* gloves for this. They look like pot holders and feel like pot scrubbers (not steel wool ones, of course). A full-body rub takes about sixty seconds for an average-size body.

For best results, brush before showering. Brush daily when you brush your teeth. When flying, brush often.

Skin brushing removes some of the static electricity we accumulate in jets. After a few weeks of regular brushing, the skin imparts a glow. The body's electrical fields have been turned up — a powerful force against accumulating anything. May the Powerful Force Against Accumulating Anything be with you!

✈ On a subtle-energy level, the touch of someone who's grounded in a timezone helps to ease jetlag. After landing, passengers met and embraced by family and friends have a headstart. Besides, who doesn't appreciate a hand with the luggage?

PAN ORAMIC WORLD AIRWAYS (View from a Jet)
Enjoying the view out the porthole of a jet speeds up jetlag recovery time. How? When we thrill at what we see, consciousness is pulled along into the present, automatically.

✈ Do not be intimidated by anyone who suggests you must close your porthole shade; it is never required.

However, if glare prevents the sleep of others, you might consider partially lowering it, or trading seats with someone on the shady side of the plane.

I have witnessed many incredible views from jets: an active volcano, the Aurora Borealis, glaciers, mountains, atolls, clouds, circular rainbows, the lights of a Japanese fishing fleet which looked like a misplaced constellation of stars, and numerous breathtaking sunrises and sunsets.

To illustrate this point, here are excerpts from my journals of these glorious natural moments.

Pink Sunrise. The effulgence which drifted towards us was diffused and dilated. It looked like a female cumulus in a tight pink dress. The pinkness parted continuously as we penetrated through, out into bright white light — a white-light sunrise finale to begin the day.

Over The Pole. Flying over the North Pole one Christmas Eve I saw the Aurora Borealis. An icicle burning like a candle? An invitation to a transcendental tree trimming?

Have you ever seen beads hanging in a doorway after someone has just walked through them? The long strands swaying back and forth at different intervals? Well, that's how Aurora looks, only on a gigantic scale.

Or, have you ever been under the ocean, snorkeling in clear tropical waters and looked back up to the surface? The light of the Sun breaks up in the water into wavy transparent spikes which undulate in rhythm with the chant of Neptune.

This Christmas Eve light appeared to rain upwards, waxing before it disappeared. Iridescent purples, yellows, greens, blues, and pinks danced in the sky for hours suspended against the black firmament.

Circular Rainbows. Three times now I've seen circular rainbows from jets — perfect concentric circles as if drawn with a giant compass.

The first time, arriving in Auckland early one a.m., I saw double, two circular rainbows, one inside the other. The inner circle had red on the outside and purple in the center, like a normal rainbow. The larger circle, however, was reversed, and paler.

Years later, somewhere over Asia, I saw another pair of rings. More relaxed this time, I watched them disappear when there were no clouds below, and reappear as clouds presented backdrops for their colors.

Recently, I saw my third set, flying in a little jet one stormy day between islands in Hawaii. Again, the colors were only visible with clouds below. And, now, wow!, in the middle of the rings was the shadow of our jet.

Refracted Sunset. Seven suns refract on the scratchy, double-ply porthole plastic. Yellow to orange to red, the seven suns slip behind a horizontal cloud envelope — and get mailed away.

Uniform. The sky became every shade of blue: teal, turquoise, and navy — like my flight-attendant uniform.

Sun Spot. We were at 40,000 feet, 30 degrees N. latitude, in summer skies. It was about 1 a.m. in Anchorage and the Sun King was bobbing on the horizon. The giant orange ball slipped off his throne, disappearing for but a moment, to enlighten distant kingdoms. Then rose on the same spot — the sun spot.

Mount Fuji. Standing in the bow of a 747, I experienced the pleasurable illusion of Mount Fuji coming to me.

Perfect Pyramid. Hilly green marked with darker patches of trees, meandering rivers, dots that are the small villages of modern Mayans, then a sprawling metropolis consumes the spaciousness of an entire verdant valley.

I float above Guatemala, through a blue cellophane bag of sterile cotton-ball clouds to the volcano, a perfect pyramid. As I glide directly over its top, I know what it is I wanted to know. Freedom isn't just flying free. It's being able to perch with a singing heart like a bird in a cage with no bars and no door.

Aspecting is a permutation on porthole viewing. This is an excellent way to help subconscious thoughts bubble up to the surface, and an exotic way to get to know yourself. The principle of aspecting, or aspect identification, is that whatever we perceive most in our environment stands out to us because it is a reflection of what we're feeling inside.

For instance, Scott came by the other day and commented on the view, specifically where the ocean meets the northern tip of Maui at Kahakuloa. "You know, that big rock out there looks just like a big round breast," are his exact words.

That particular rock had always reminded me of old *stupa* temples I had seen in India, places way out in the country overgrown with vegetation, and with a statue of a god inside.

Here's another example of aspecting. Today, as I was starting my yoga practice I looked at the sky, and the cloud which caught my eye resembled a giant fork. *What could this mean*, I asked myself. *Oh, I want to eat*, immediately popped into my mind. So I addressed the part of me which would prefer to eat than exercise, *Yes, dear, we'll have a nice breakfast after yoga*.

Aspecting is a fun way to bridge the subconscious mind with the conscious one. It's especially easy with clouds, and the window of a jet is the perfect place to get started.

As we dialogue with our subconscious, we can address worries or concerns not known to us before. And we can ask the subconscious for help in this process. For instance, *What does this mean?*, if we see an aspect we don't understand. The answer may come in an intuitive flash, as mine did in the example above. Or sometimes we need to look back out, for more insights. Trust the subconscious to have some answers or solutions and

look for them through this new porthole to your self —
this window of the mind.

LET YOUR SPIRIT SOAR (Meditation)

Scientists who study the relationship of meditation to
the human body have noted numerous positive side-
effects, such as lowered blood pressure and increased
amounts of alpha waves in the brain (indicating relaxation). Even *The New York Times*[41] reported that a
lifestyle change, including daily meditation, can
"reverse heart disease without drugs or surgery."

As our bodies heal through a daily meditation practice, our outlook improves, too. It's as if a clenched fist
relaxes into an open hand. The former represents a person who is contracted in on self, possibly with self-pity,
or indulgence; the latter is the gesture of a receptive
person, one capable of a firm handshake — and
applause.

The word "meditation," in today's parlance, covers a
wide variety of exercises. Two forms have helped me
when traveling. The first practice involves focusing on
a specific field of inquiry — for example, packing.

✦ Packing Meditation (investment: thirty minutes). A
few days prior to departure, close your eyes and imagine
you are sitting in front of a large, silver movie screen.
Now, start your movie. *See* yourself fulfilling your travel
plans in the future: leaving for the airport, in flight, in
your hotel room, sightseeing, eating, meetings. Whom
do you meet? What do you wear? Ah-ha!

✦ Close your meditation by thanking your Place of
Advance Clear Knowing (PACK) for this information.
Then, follow through: put the items you have *seen* into
your travel bags.

✦ Additionally, at this point, you may want to ask yourself, Where I'm going what are the local customs?

Travelers occasionally encounter disrespect when dress violates local mores. We hear of western women who fend off rape attempts and western men who scare off business deals because they dress too casually.

Arab women certainly understand this caution. Often, they'll board flights in the West wearing designer clothes and jewelry. Then, shortly before touchdown in Riyadh, for example, they'll pull out black veils from carry-ons and cover themselves from head to toe.

In the East, the veil has been, since time immemorial, a symbol of consciousness. Removing a veil specifically equates with dropping any old belief which can numb us and dissociate us from the truth.

Removing veils of consciousness is the purpose of the second form of meditation which I wish to introduce here. ✈ Sit quietly, with your eyes closed, and look into the inner blackness. Calmly watch and hear as thoughts come and go like vehicles on a freeway. We can follow one home, or anywhere. Or we can choose to let it go. Let it all go. Going, going, gone.

Here is where Meditation begins. This is not a thinking place — but Being. It's the Well from where all well-being springs.

When we picture the twenty-four timezones around our Earth, we see that all the lines converge at the Poles. At the North Pole, for example, every time on Earth can be told at once — revealing the mind-boggling concept of no time at all.

Daily Meditation is the way to find one's own inner True North — the place to where time flies.

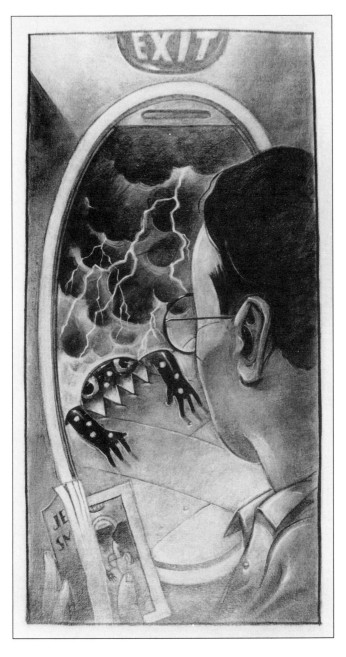

Stalking the Dragon

COMPLICATING DISCOMBOBULATION

THE AIRBORNE HABITAT (Compounding Jetlag)
In 1980, Mr. Springbett, on a $10,000 bet, broke the world record for "fastest circling of the earth by commercial airlines."[42] He flew the Concorde one leg, changed planes five times, and spent $8,000 on air fares. "What a case of jetlag!" people said.

Not really. After two days and nights almost entirely airborne, Springbett had landed right back where he started, on the same timezone — so he couldn't have suffered jetlag. However, I bet he came down with an acute case of *jet-snag.*

Jet-snag is what I'm calling the specific effects of the inflight environment — a place which can be high in radiation, ozone, electromagnetic (EM) pulses, noise, and contaminants while low in oxygen, pressure, and humidity. Thus, a person flying, for example, from Boston to Bogota, never leaves his timezone and never crosses the equator; nevertheless, he is still at the effect of these unnatural forces.

Jet-snag compounds jetlag, both in depth and in

duration, and is especially critical to those travelers with a medical condition. For example, "A study showed that 6-7% of people with certain ischemic [lack of blood to an organ] heart disease die after they travel by air."[43]

To assist passengers in taking all necessary steps to prevent and/or remedy the deleterious jet-snag, I continue to offer practical tips gleaned from my decades of global orbits. I am also introducing, at the end of the next six chapters which address the multiple and diverse aspects of jet-snag, a subtle-energy coping strategy: affirmation.

Affirmation is a synonym for *positive mental attitude* in business management and sales. In medicine, the concept is known as psycho-neuro-immunology. I call it Dragon Wisdom because I learned it from dragonflies.

Living at cloud level, as I now do, many dragonflies become, inadvertently, trapped in my cottage. When trapped, dragonflies *zhapp* their wings for hours on the windows, as they desperately seek freedom.

One day, offhandedly, I said to such a victim, *If you need assistance, just step on my finger.*

It did!

Since then I have carried many dragonflies to freedom. In the early days, I used to say, as they stepped on board, *Don't worry.* On the word *worry*, each one flew off. When I saw the pattern, I got it: the word *worry* has a negative vibration, and dragonflies are sensitive to the subtle energies of words!

So are we.

You will find a Dragon Wisdom at the end of each of the next six chapters to help counterbalance the negative vibrations of jet-snag. For best results, reaffirm each one several times, silently or out loud.

FLYING HIGH AND FEELING LOW

DROWNING IN MID AIR (Altitude)

Jets cruise at altitudes between twenty-five and sixty thousand feet. At these Olympian heights, there is not enough oxygen in the atmosphere for passengers to breathe. Aircraft designers, of course, developed a way for us to sit, talk, and eat on board without using oxygen masks.

Jet engines (made by Rolls-Royce and other high-powered companies) compress (pressurize) outside air before pumping it into the cabins. This creates the breathable, though "thin," aircraft air, comparable, in this sense, to the atmosphere of high-mountain locales.

For instance, a jet cruising at 35,000 feet has an interior altitude of 5,500 feet. Those at 40,000 approximate the height of Mexico City, 7,500 feet. Theoretically, if you are flying to Mexico City while eating tacos and sipping a Corona, apparent altitudinal differences will be minimal!

The shift to high altitudes, however, is hard on the body. When the 1968 Olympic Games were held in

Mexico City, world-class athletes had to train for its unusually high altitude.

What can we jetters do to train? The first thing is to be aware that high altitude air has low pressure, and this alters our bodies in odd ways. For example, all our tissues swell up with nitrogen gas[44] expanding about 20 per cent at 5000 feet (interior altitude), 25 per cent at 6,000 feet, and 35 per cent at 8,000 feet.[45]

Most passengers first notice this when their feet swell on board. After they've kicked off their shoes, they find that they can't get the darn things back on.

✈ Buy travel shoes which are half a size too big. Use cushion inserts for ground wear; then at cruise altitude take out the inserts for another perfect fit.

Another little-known place which can swell up is a dental filling. My dentist maintains that years of frequent, sudden altitude changes has actually loosened all my fillings!

For some travelers, inflight air can even cause a tooth to explode! Teeth which explode in flight are generally those with amalgam fillings in which a bubble of air or moisture has been inadvertently left by a dentist. Gold and ceramics are less likely to blow because they're made in sterile labs. So, now you know. If your stewardess drops her dentures on your tray, you'll be able to say, "I understand, the pressures of the job have gotten to you!"

Some dentists advise, avoid dental work immediately before air travel to prevent aerondontalgia, jetters' toothache. I've often had work done on layovers in Tokyo, though, and have never had this problem. It's best to ask your dentist.

Rarefied air on jets is not quite what most of us are used to, unless we were born and bred in places like Tibet, the Andes, the Himalayas, or the Ethiopian highlands, where genetic adaptations have changed residents' lungs (larger) and capillaries (more and wider).[46] The rest of us may need to take special care at high altitude.

✈ Those travelers with specific health conditions which may be impacted by low air pressure (such as cardiovascular, pulmonary, or gastro-intestinal weakness, multiple chemical sensitivities, and pregnancy) would be well served to consult, prior to flight, a physician familiar with aviation medicine.

✈ In any event, it's best to check with your own physician regarding medications in relation to timezone shifts. In this regard I was told that certain prescriptions, i.e., estrogen, need to be taken at regular intervals to be effective; others must be ingested at specific times of the day, i.e., blood-pressure medicine in the p.m. or diuretics in the a.m. Still others, such as insulin, require different adjustments of dosage when flying east or flying west.[47]

Another bizarre note in this chronicle of low air pressure concerns women with breast implants. *The Journal of the American Medical Association* reports that, "Any air in the breast implant expands to twice its size."[48]

Fingers swell, too. Many passengers take off their rings on board, and some lose expensive jewelry this way. Once a passenger lost an emerald ring. She thought she'd left it on her dinner tray. Sad to say, the attendants had already dumped all the garbage and stacked the trays. In order to locate the missing jewel, the crew had to empty all the garbage bins, which had been filled to the brim with coffee, chicken bones, gravy, and other inflight refuse, and pour all this swill onto the galley floor.

Two flight attendants were down on hands and knees

feeling though this stuff-that-humans-waste, when a passenger walked by on his way to the lav. He watched for a while, and finally asked with a voice full of helium, "What are you doing?"

The first flight attendant, equipped with a quick brain (as well as a strong stomach) looked up and quipped, "We're hunting for an emerald, sir. We're trying to find the glamour in this job."

✈ To avoid losing precious rings and other jewelry on board, bring a dedicated zippered case to use in flight after your body expands. This zippered case is also useful, after landing, for storing valuables in your hotel safe.

✈ When we travel with valuables, even if we don't lose something, we often pay with peace of mind. *Can I travel with expensive things and still maintain well-being?* This is a question to pose yourself when you first start packing.

Airlines say they are not capable of creating an interior altitude equivalent to sea level. Nor would they want to.

Sea-level air weight would impose greater pressure on the fuselage (the aircraft's skin), result in heavier planes, impact a jet's ability to get off the ground, and require extra fuel. At present, airlines carry passengers, baggage, and a payload of cargo instead of just sea-level air.

Therefore, passengers get less oxygen to breathe. In reaction, passengers often, unconsciously, take only shallow breaths, and this is counter-productive.

✈ Conscious breathing, exerting awareness and muscular strength to inhale/exhale fully and deeply, helps get more oxygen to the brain to maintain well-being. Inhale/exhale to a set count, i.e., four seconds in, four seconds out. Count as high as you can; yogis are known to count to sixty! Conscious breathing is effective in flight, during transits, and especially after landing, right before sleep.

✈ Use conscious sighing to help clear emotions: inhale fully, then exhale, sighing. Repeat as necessary.

Passengers experience the reduced air pressure on jets through a variety of signals. As this relates to hypoxia (oxygen starvation), see BOTTOM LINE VS LIFELINE, page 73. As regards anemia, see PUFF THE TRAGIC DRAG, page 97. With respect to ear problems, see NO POP, page 104. Concerning a decompression, see 18 SECONDS, page 106.

One final note about inflight low air pressure as it affects those who spend a great deal of time in the airborne habitat: 99% of flight attendants have, at one time or another, suffered hemorrhoids in the line of duty. ✈ Pinch Pennies. Imagine you are pinching a penny between your buttocks. Pull in your coin slot (inhale). Release (exhale). Do this anytime and often on your travel day, sitting or standing.

TO PEE OR NOT TO PEE (Dehydration)
Inflight cabin air is dryer than any of the world's deserts. Typically, relative humidity (the moisture content of the air) is 20-25% in the Sahara or Arabian deserts, while optimum comfort is around 50-55%.[49] "Inflight cabin humidities gradually fall on long-distance, high-altitude flights to well below 10%, in many cases approaching 1%."[50] What moisture is left in the passengers' cabins is simply your and my perspirations and exhalations. Thus, the more crowded the plane, the more humid it remains, and the more we flyers *merge* by inhaling extracts of each other.

The bottom line is this: dehydration rates increase two- to three-fold in the jet environment. "Dehydration occurs commonly although most people aren't aware of some of the subtle signs. In normal conditions we exhale approximately 20% of our water intake. Aboard long flights this figure will rise to almost 50%."[51] In extreme cases, when a body gets dehydrated, the brain sends an SOS to the kidneys, which then reabsorb water from our own urine. This sets in motion a radical state of affairs involving "at least 100 biochemical and hormonal rhythms in the body"[52] including, paradoxically, fluid retention.

One of the first symptoms of dehydration, which most passengers notice after flying, is dry skin. Even Miss America 1991, Marjorie Vincent, gets "those little lines around her eyes after she's been in the air for hours."[53]

Other bodily signals of dehydration include light-headedness, headache, and dry, itchy, red eyes.

It doesn't do for crew to have bloodshot eyes, and many resort to eye drops to remove those telltale streaks through the sky of the eye. I used drops for about ten years or so, until I decided to break the addiction. Now, when I fly, I prefer to use a thick eyecream.

✈ Use of a thick eyecream around the borders of eyes helps them retain their moisture.

✈ Use of water mist around eyes also helps them to retain their moisture. Close eyes and *spritz* entire face with water, using a travel-size, empty perfume atomizer, refilled on board with your drinking water.

✈ For humidified breathing air: cover your nose and mouth with a water-saturated large cotton hanky. Fold on the diagonal and wrap ends around ears.

The speed with which moisture evaporates from this hanky will give you some idea of the degree of the aircraft's dryness. On twelve-hour flights, for example, a passenger may want to wet the hanky a dozen or so times for a comfortable humidity. As an experiment, you can also try bringing a wet swim suit or just-washed lingerie in your carry-on. Hang it out a few hours after takeoff when all the humidity from the ground is gone. Drying is accomplished in an hour or so at cruise altitude. The same garment takes at least twenty-four hours to fully dry, for example, in Tokyo or New York.

Today, the technology for humidifying jets is readily available; such equipment is an option at Boeing, for instance. In addition to the initial expense of hardware, however, the extra weight of water on takeoff (to create humidity later when airborne) is, most likely, what commercial carriers consider prohibitive. For example, to sustain a relative humidity of 35%, a 747 will need to weigh 2200 pounds (1000 kgs.) more on takeoff[54] — translating into about fifteen passengers left at the gate!

Doctors recommend that active, healthy adults drink eight ounces (250ml) of water eight times a day. Crew are advised by airline medical to drink eight ounces of water per hour of flighttime. I like to drink twice that amount, of purified or mineral water, when traveling.

For passengers, ironically, airline beverage carts do not abound with a fine selection of the world's choice mineral waters. In fact, they offer drinks which seem to compound jetlag, such as carbonated soft drinks, canned juices, coffee, and tea. Carbonated soft drinks can cause intestinal gas, because all gases expand at high altitudes. Moreover, their sugar content can intensify low blood sugar levels, which are already a concern as our adrenals try to race into new timezones. Canned juices usually contain quite a bit of salt and, in flight, excess salt intensifies the swollen-feet-and-legs syndrome. Orange juice could be a good occasional choice, but it's usually prepared on board, using one part canned to three parts tap. Here's the scoop on the tap: there are no standards for commercial aircraft water tanks, for cleanliness, treatment procedures, nor water quality in cities around the world where commercial jets refill.

Most airlines have mechanics fill water tanks as needed; then, to wipe out parasites and bacteria, they're told to add chlorine and bicarbonate of soda to "sanitize and sweeten" (to taste?). Air France is the only honest airline that I know of, in this regard; they post signs informing passengers "the tap is not potable." Ice, by the way, is made on the ground, where its water source may still be questionable.

The airlines also proffer coffee and tea at every service. These beverages, unfortunately, have diuretic properties, making the reality of inflight dehydration even more intense.

✈ However, for those passengers still interested, here's how to get the hottest cup of coffee available in the sky: walk back to a galley yourself and ask a flight attendant to give you *freshly-made hot coffee in a paper crew cup.*

Cold coffee is a problem in jets because, at high altitudes, coffee boils at about 180 degrees F., instead of the normal 212 degrees, and because the porcelain and plastic cups used to serve it are usually refrigerated alongside perishable food.

Today's airline beverage services also, unfortunately, give passengers the false idea that drinking alcohol is a good thing to do while jetting. Beverage carts overflow with cute little alcohol miniatures in all manner of shapes. ✈ Frequent flyers know that alcohol and altitude are not compatible.

Alcohol poisons the tissue cells so that we cannot utilize oxygen properly. With the already reduced oxygen supply in jets, this ill effect is even more pronounced.[55]

In fact, alcohol doesn't belong in the air. This is particularly true for crew, of course. Not too long ago you may have read about three pilots convicted of the felony of drunk flying.[56] Their inept defense maintained that the flight was "perfectly routine." The FAA countermanded with "eight hours from bottle to throttle," citing sixteen jet crashes tied to pilot substance abuse.[57]

I don't want you to get the idea that it is unsafe to fly. All the pilots I've met are responsible, disciplined people. If anything goes wrong on an airplane, I have total confidence that commercial pilots will rise to the occasion.

Check out your pilots yourself, if you wish. You can meet your airmen and airwomen (about 2% of commercial pilots are female)[58] as follows:

✈ It is permissible for passengers to visit the flight deck before (but never during) flight. Board as early as possible. Then, make your way toward the nose of the jet (and up the stairs on a 747). The cockpit door is usually open on the ground. If not, query the closest attendant, *I'd love to see the cockpit.*

The cockpit, by the way, is really something to behold with its hundreds of switches, dials, flashing lights, and musical tones. For instance, there are five different sounds to alert pilots of danger; each corresponds to a colored, flashing light on the instrument panel. A steady horn, for example, blows when air pressure reaches 14,000 feet, danger altitude. A wailer means the automatic pilot has disconnected. The harmonic tone warns the jet is 1000 feet off the assigned altitude. A chirping cricket indicates that the wings may fall off. (Somebody has a weird sense of humor. You'd think a bugle playing *Taps* would be more appropriate if the wings were about to fall off!)

Ask the pilots to play these sounds for you — they do it for visiting kids and other dignitaries.

Most people now believe that the consumption of a lot of water is the first and foremost remedy for jetlag. In fact, it is helpful for jetlag; however, I feel it's more directly related to jet-snag — to the experience of dehydration in jets.

✈ Jet dehydration is essentially remedied by drinking eight to sixteen ounces of water per hour of flying. The longer the flight, the more water needed, exponentially.

✈ One exception to the drink-all-you-can-when-jetting rule pertains to drinking with meals. Liquids with meals dilute digestive juices, thus contributing to intestinal swelling.

✈ If you want to follow only one piece of advice in this book, this would be it. Carry your own bottled water on board as a backup in case the airplane runs out.

On board, there is rarely enough bottled water for all those who want it, as supplies have not kept pace with the demand. Occasionally, on long-hauls, aircraft run dry altogether — no water for coffee, or even for flushing. It's smart to be prepared: have your own water in reserve.

✈ Request a full can of water during bar and meal services; save your own supply for later and for transit stops.

✈ Carbonated or plain? Sometimes, carbonated helps balance intestinal gas. Plain is usually most satisfying in thin air.

✈ Smart-class passengers walk back to a galley about once an hour to combat dehydration and muscle atrophy. Ask any attendant there to fix you a drink. If your preference is non-alcoholic ask permission to make it yourself.

I can hear your unspoken concerns.

Will flight attendants resent this overt independence on the part of passengers? No — although, at first, they may act surprised. In fact, as long-hauls drag on, they will probably begin to show with smiles and friendly conversation that they truly appreciate one less passenger to fetch and carry for.

Doesn't self service contradict airline marketing, which competitively boasts the desire to pamper passengers? No. These ads reveal only fluid tongues. No commercial airline I know is adequately staffed to serve everyone this quantity of bottled water, even in first class. For example, on long-hauls of fifteen hours, three services are it.

What if everybody were to rise to the occasion at the same time? Wouldn't it cause the plane to tip over? No. Jumbo jets are not gondolas.

✈ Prolific liquid intake on board usually leads to multiple visits to lavs. These trips are not in vain. You won't suffer dehydration, you'll get a little exercise, and queuing up time and again, you'll meet those of like mind — the jet-smart set!

After landing, urine output is one of the indicators doctors use to assess dehydration. None during the night and heavy flow early morning is considered normal.

✈ Untimely nighttime urges to urinate can be used as a barometer of dehydration and jetlag; i.e., when untimely urges cease, you know, at last, you're clear.

Note: Urinating at night because you ate or drank right before sleep is a different matter altogether.

✈ Post flight, it's important to remember to continue drinking a lot of water for several days.

Bathing, when dehydrated, helps to replenish moisture right through the pores. Bathing also relaxes the nervous system from the stressors, jetlag and jet-snag.

✈ As soon as possible after jetting submerge in water — in an ocean, a river, a pool, or a tub.

✈ Take several baths your first day after long-hauls.

✈ Be held by someone in water. Have them float you clockwise in the Northern Hemisphere, and counter-clockwise Down Under, just the way water goes down the drain in these locales. See if this feels good to you and do whatever feels best.

➤ A tub full of water also helps humidify air-conditioned hotel rooms when you don't drain, especially useful after flying to dry locales such as Saudi Arabia. Running a shower for five minutes can also help.

➤ When checking into a hotel, request a room with a tub, not just a shower. In Hong Kong, for example, hotels have extra-large, real porcelain tubs, where you can totally submerge. This is especially therapeutic after jetting.

➤ Therapeutic Bathing Ritual:

Step One: Close the stopper and turn on all the hot water, full force. The splashing waterfall aerates and effervesces the tub with oxygen-rich bubbles.

Step Two: Add epsom salts, and/or handfuls of baking soda and sea salt. Check temperature. Add cold if necessary.

Step Three: Lie full length in tub. Close eyes. Submerge. Underwater, I hold my breath for as long as I can. I'm always different after I re-surface; either my aura or my thought patterns — something about me has been changed by the total immersion. Relax in the tub for a while longer; exercise under water. Let the mind fly.

Step Four: Remain in tub while draining water; consciously send jetlag down and out with it. Say to your jetlag, "I send you down the drain! *Adieu. Sayonara.*"

Step Five: Finish with a cold shower. This is important and easier than you think after a hot bath. The Swedes jump in the snow after sauna! A cold shower is a must to close pores and reinvigorate energy flow.

On one layover in Hong Kong, my therapeutic bathing ritual turned into a wet event! That day, after submerging with eyes closed I resurfaced, inhaled deeply, and — there, bending over me, was the Chinese roomboy in his conspicuous blue and gold uniform! "Missy, you all right?" he asked.

Probably he had knocked (underwater I can't hear anything) and, thinking I was out, had let himself in to tidy up. I screamed, "Ahghh," and he ran away.

With inadequate water intake, health and inspiration can quickly stagnate. Water is about 55% of our body mass, researchers say. In infancy it's closer to 75%, we're told, while the proportion drops to about 40% when we get old. The thought that looking old might have something to do with not drinking enough water can really motivate some people (of course, I mean me).

Dragon Wisdom
I count my Blessings and do my best. I have faith that the Almighty Pilot takes care of the rest.

Now We're Cooking

ZAP! (Radiation)

Commercial jets take advantage of jetstreams to save fuel and time. Ironically, "concentrations of cosmic radiation in jetstreams, precisely where commercial jets fly, is two times as high as just above or below the jetstream."[59]

In fact, radiation exposure for passengers flying between New York and London, for example, is about the same as a chest X-ray and, according to experts, will increase a person's risk of getting cancer.[60]

Since most harmful radiation in jets originates from the Sun, some scientists suspect there's less at night. Others say that too little research has been done to know for sure. They all agree, however, that radiation is cumulative. It comes to us not only from the Sun, but also from nuclear power production and accidents, bomb-testing fallout, X-rays, radar, smoke detectors, and radiopharmaceuticals.[61] Even before we board a flight, the food in our carry-ons is exposed to radiation at security. Today, only the Concorde is equipped to measure inflight radiation exposures, and its crews are the only ones keeping cumulative logs. As a matter of fact, airline crews receive higher radiation doses than those incurred in almost any other industry.[62]

To neutralize radiation exposures, I take a supplement, SOD (superoxide dismutase and catalase) made by Biotec and found in healthfood stores. SOD is known as "the radiation antidote" because of its ability to repair cells damaged by radiation.[63] Research started on SOD in 1939; it would take a biochemist (I am not one) to explain about free radical pathology: how unpaired electrons get neutralized by SOD.

✈ I start taking SOD about a week before departure, on an empty stomach and always with a large glass of water.

I was introduced to SOD by a California nutritionist in '83 when I was on the Los Angeles/London route. At the time I'd flown about two hundred of these trips over the Pole, landing at Heathrow at dawn — one of the worst possible routes for jetlag. It was a fairly controlled situation, though, a perfect one for an experiment in remedies: same aircraft, flighttime, timezones, and hotel. (Only the faces and the headrest covers changed.) On my first trip with SOD, I felt a marked improvement in my well-being.

At this point, the only radiation advice from scientists is this: during solar flares (proton events) when exposures can jump hundreds of times: 1) pregnant women should not fly[64] and, 2) orbiting astronauts should stay inside their shielded craft. Commercial jets are not shielded, due to weight restrictions.

Passengers who want to take more precautions should consider radiation exposure when choosing their flights, as this relates to routing, altitude, and aircraft type.

Routing: "The radiation level over the polar regions at air carrier cruise altitudes is about twice that over the equator at the same altitudes."[65]

Altitude: "Inflight exposure rates actually double every 6,500 feet (2,000 meters)."[66]

Aircraft type: Higher-altitude commercial jets include the Concorde, Boeings 747SP, 747-400, 767-300ER, Airbus A340-200, and some MD-11s which have auxiliary fuel tanks.

Additionally, passengers may want to cancel their travel plans during proton events. Proton information can be accessed at the Space Environment Services Center (303/497-3235), on a daily updated one-minute recording. Joe Hirman, its manager, told me that about sixty of these events occur every eleven years in peaks; '91 -'93 is an example of such a peak.

Another source of toxic radiation exposure for passengers and crew is found in commercial jet cargo holds. "In the United States during 1975, radioactive material was transported on about 1 of every 30 passenger flights. Since 1975 there was a slight decrease in the number of packages of radioactive material transported by air."[67] Passengers concerned about onboard radiation exposure might consider lobbying against this practice.

The only positive side of aviation radiation I can think of is the Aurora Borealis. This awesome display of cosmic lights can occasionally be seen out portholes on polar flights, and is actually radiation in action. (See Pan Oramic World Airways, page 43.)

OH! ZONED (Ozone)

Ozone gas is present at the altitudes commercial jets fly, particularly in the spring in the Northern Hemisphere and in the fall in the Southern Hemisphere. Do not assume just because the internal environment of a jet is encapsulated that there is no danger from atmospheric ozone. It enters right through the cabin air-conditioning system.[68] Sealed aircraft are, presently, only available to astronauts.

Though most ozone remains in the ozonosphere 20-30 miles up, wisps of it stray down to the altitudes jets fly. Like radiation, the higher we fly, the more ozone we find.

Not only are humans damaging the ozone layer, but *it* is also harmful to us! The ozone we encounter in flight is a gas with the potential to burn up tissue, depending on its concentration in the air we breathe, the length of time we are exposed, and the amount of activity a person engages in when exposed. Most probably this is why it was the union of flight attendants who first started screaming (with hoarse voices) about the problem. Due to the aerobic nature of this work, flight attendants inhale about four times as much ozone as anyone else on board.[69]

Today, scientists differ in their opinions about present inflight solutions for ozone. Some believe the catalytic converters which have been installed adequately turn ozone into oxygen. Others say it's still a problem because the catalytic filters are not effective "when the engines are throttled back before descent."[70]

Signals of ozone poisoning include cough, headache, burning eyes, and pain taking in full breaths.[71] A flight attendant health survey conducted in 1984 showed that 62% of respondents experienced these symptoms.[72] "In 1978-1979, the FAA monitored ozone on flights (mostly at 30,000-40,000 feet) and found that 11% were in violation of the FAA's ozone concentration limits."[73]

In 1976, the 747SP (special performance) jet inaugurated service, and my co-workers and I experienced ozone for the first time. The SP is a shorter version 747 with extra fuel tanks and fewer seats. It cruises around 46,000 feet, instead of the usual 35,000 feet. The Concorde soars even higher, around 60,000 feet, where the threat of ozone and radiation contamination is greater still.

Concordephiles, however, claim that dangers at this altitude are offset by the supersonic's reduced flighttime. Concordephobes retort that the supersonic's high-altitude emissions of nitric oxide cause more damage to the ozone layer than all the fluorocarbons deployed on Earth.

STOP BUGGING ME (Airborne Contaminants)

Another hornet's nest for passengers traveling in commercial jets is the likelihood of microbial contamination due to the low content of fresh air on board. Most jets provide only 40% to 60% fresh air; the rest is recirculated, usually through a particle filter that does not remove germs.[74]

During the colder months, "frequent flyers complain nonstop of upper respiratory tract infections."[75] "Severe infections are almost inevitable sequelae to intercontinental air travel presumably from prolonged recirculation of mixed viruses from 450 people in a confined area."[76] Moreover, fatigue from travel and jetlag makes us all the more prone to catching infections.

Airborne, biologically-derived particles include bacteria, viruses, and fungal spores. All can be present in aircraft cabins. Anything smaller than arthropod fragments (pieces of bugs) is not likely to be caught by the aircraft filters.

For passengers subjected to long delays after boarding, long runway taxis, and non-disembarking transit stops, the risk of infection is exponentially increased. During these times the cabin air is usually not ventilated at all!

Documentation of contagious illness aboard commercial aircraft is rare for two reasons: 1) dispersion of passengers after arrival and, 2) incubation time.

Dispersion: One incident of transmission of contagious disease aboard a commercial jet was documented because the passengers did not disperse. The aircraft had a mechanical problem at a small airport. All passengers were kept on board for four hours without air-conditioning before the flight was cancelled. The only doctor in town reported that one person had the flu at the onset of the delay; within three days, 72% of the passengers were complaining of cough, fever, fatigue, headache, and sore throat.[77]

Incubation: Although one week usually suffices to resynchronize the body after jetting, two weeks or more is required before we have the ability to respond to a toxic challenge.[78]

Notwithstanding incubation time, I experienced such a transmission one nightflight Down Under. About six hours into the flight, my throat swelled up, and, within moments, five passengers complained to me of the same. Alarmed, I reported to the cockpit. The captain informed me, indeed, there was a severely ill child on board; though the airlines normally refuse boarding to such passengers, that night the captain had been personally petitioned and had made an exception.

The effects of someone spreading a contagious disease are not even confined to a single flight. Aircraft interiors can be contaminated for many days; respiratory droplets, spread by coughing, sneezing, even talking, accumulate on bulkhead panels, upholstered seats, and circulation systems. On takeoff, spores jostle about like participants at a Brazilian Mardi Gras. They take to the air in microscopic clouds, then circulate among the passengers and crew.

Commercial aircraft are rarely disinfected. Like Brazilian playboys from the above-mentioned Mardi Gras, they are constantly on the move and very elusive. They remain, primarily, in transit, stopping in airports only long enough for teams of cleaners — actually, tidiers — to race through their chores under pressure of time constraints.

✈ To help prevent microbial contamination on jets, keep your hands away from eyes, nose, and mouth. Also, wash your hands frequently with soap and hot water. And, afterwards, to prevent dryness, moisturize them with cream or a light oil.

"Although the low relative humidities present in most aircraft during flight can be deadly for some bacteria, such conditions probably augment the viability of most viruses."[79] Some scientists say that viruses penetrate our immune system through the tiny cracks inside our nostrils, and that this is intensified in jets by dehydration whereby the tiny cracks get raw and enlarged.

✈ Reduce your chances of catching infections on jets by coating the inside of your nostrils with a light oil.

In 1986 the U.S. government Committee on Airline Cabin Air Quality recommended that a regulation be established requiring removal of passengers on the ground within thirty minutes of ventilation failure, because of the "likelihood of occurrence of epidemic disease when forced-air ventilation is not available."[80]

✈ While we wait for this regulation, we can, individually and collectively, ask to disembark after thirty minutes of ventilation failure citing *The Airliner Cabin Environment* study, published by the National Academy Press.

Whether or not we are permitted to disembark in such a circumstance is still a question which remains up in the air. Each carrier has its individual policies; and responsibility for this decision rests with each captain.

Dragon Wisdom

Only feelings of peace and security enter me through the air waves and the All Ways.

THE BUDGET MONSTER

BOTTOM LINE VS LIFELINE (Fuel Saving)
Since deregulation in 1978, when the U.S. government loosened its hold on airline regulations, increased competition among carriers has given rise to many *cost-effective* moves. The most insidious is the reduction of passengers' air in an effort to conserve fuel. This is similar to the way a car owner, for example, turns off the air-conditioner to save on gas. In cars, of course, the air-conditioner is essentially a comfort device. In jets, however, it functions for life support.[81]

In spite of this, 747 pilots, for example, routinely turn off one third of the passengers' airflow, while they (the pilots) enjoy an oxygen-rich cockpit. Ventilation for a pilot is actually ten times that of an economy passenger.[82]

Scientists have now proven that impaired vision is one of the symptoms of rarefied air.[83] The airlines, in their wisdom, of course, want to ensure that pilots can see. I've heard from pilots that airlines offer them bonuses when they implement this fuel-saving measure. I believe these pilots sincerely don't fathom what a difference it makes to the well-being of those of us in the cabins. I clearly experience more jetlag signals, especially body aches and lightheadedness, after flights when an air pack (there are three on every 747) has been deactivated, or when one or two are inoperable. Full working airflow is not even required for takeoff clearance.

Turning off one air pack saves the airlines approximately $80/hour in jet fuel, I was told by a pilot. This same airman showed me the three toggle switches on the cockpit instrument panel which govern this function.

Feeling flushed with a clammy sweat always alerted me, almost immediately, when a pack was deactived. I used to go right up to the cockpit to verify my perception with the toggles' position. Many pilots expressed to me that they felt I was meddling, so I got to carrying in a fresh pitcher of water, or leftovers from a first-class hors d'oeuvres cart, just to check it out.

Some doctors will go so far as to say that all of us riding in the cabins of commercial jets today suffer mild hypoxia, decreased oxygen in the central nervous system. Hypoxia signals are similar to those of mountain sickness: lightheadedness, shallow breathing, and fatigue.[84]

Flight attendants are usually the first to notice a diminished airflow due to their aerobic activities.[85]

Passengers, on the other wing, may not put two and two together, because of the other symptoms of hypoxia: euphoria (like an alcohol high) and inability to concentrate (chiefly in math and new tasks). In flight, this can lead to multiple misadventures for the unknowing business-person trying to concentrate on spreadsheets and expense reports.

✦ Help hypoxic attendants by offering exact change for inflight headsets, drinks, and dutyfree purchases.

✈ Deep-sea divers may also be among the first to notice a reduction in airflow. Early signals of the bends (which can occur aloft if flying less than twenty-four hours after diving) are headache and joint pain. In this event, the pilot should be notified immediately; if a lower altitude is not assumed the passenger could die.

Some airlines' policy is that all air packs are only utilized after someone complains. When I complained while on duty, I was told by management that "someone" did not include a flight attendant.

Many passengers notice the diminished oxygen in the cabin, but they don't speak up until after landing. Commercial airlines' ventilation/temperature was rated "less than good" by 21% of 140,000 readers of *Consumer Reports* in 1990.[86]

✈ It's always important to tell a flight attendant if you experience difficulty breathing. This may also result from a slow decompression (a loss of pressure from a leaky door, a crack in the fuselage, or a faulty outflow valve). "Several reports of U.S. airline aircraft cabin pressure malfuctions are received by the FAA each month."[87]

✈ If you feel clammy and/or stuffy on board, ask a flight attendant to convey this information to the cockpit, specifically mentioning you'd like *full utilization of air*.

✈ If you ever feel that your breaths are shallow and labored, ask a flight attendant for an oxygen bottle. There are about twenty-five portable bottles, for example, on every 747 and you don't need to be gasping to get one.

You might say something like, *I feel like I'm having difficulty breathing. May I have some oxygen, please?*

✈ When any passenger uses oxygen, everyone three rows forward, aft, and across cannot smoke. The pilots will also be notified; most probably, they'll amp up the air flow.

When a passenger is having trouble breathing, the pilot may also illuminate the no-smoking sign and instruct the flight attendants to check throughout the aircraft, to make sure that the lower-sidewall-floor-level vents are clear and not blocked by carry-on bags.

"Are there any important advantages in flying first class? I believe there are none," wrote the World Bank's Health Director. "Consider how much money could be saved and used in more productive ways if most of us gave up first-class travel."[88] I have to disagree with the doctor. First class is not about gourmet fare; it's about air — approximately three times more per passenger than in economy.[89]

Perhaps it will take large numbers of us asking for the portable bottles to convince the airlines to provide us all with a richer blend. Let's not hold our breath, though!

In the meantime, some entrepreneur might consider oxygen booths in airports. A few good gulps after landing would help with jetlag, as the Japanese have already noted with oxygen vending machines aiding city dwellers to alleviate metropolitan hypoxia.

✈ If you're looking for oxygen after landing and your airport doesn't provide it, stop by a dive shop. Otherwise, you have to have a doctor's prescription.

I'm an experienced oxygen sipper; for many years while working in jets I availed myself of the portable bottles (the same ones I suggest you ask for), as well as cockpit oxygen on tap (only when invited by compassionate pilots). Over and over again I noted, after fifteen minutes or so of breathing pure oxygen, that my skin was not so thin any more. I could again convert yen into dollars, dullards into conversationalists, and my own gray cheeks into the pink blush of enthusiasm.

Having difficulty breathing due to stuffy air is different
from needing supplemental oxygen prescribed for a specific medical condition. For this, each airline has indi-
vidualized policies.[90] Notwithstanding, passengers are
never permitted to bring their own bottles; if one
should drop and break its neck, it could fly though the
air, and even pierce a fuselage.

✈ The airlines will provide supplemental oxygen for a
surcharge; request, in advance, through reservations.

Since deregulation, airlines have implemented many
cost-effective procedures in order to cut the competitive
corner: removing ashtrays on no-smoking sectors to
lighten weight; replacing butter with margarine and
cream with "dry whitener"; canceling flights at the last
minute when only light loads have booked; refusing to
make onward connections for passengers when flights
get diverted; delaying commencement of the cabin air-
conditioning system on the ground until the last minute
before passengers' boarding; even neglecting to regularly
clean cabin air filters. More often than not, these filters
are gummy with debris much like old Notre Dame de
Paris, crumbling in the face of this century's petro-
chemical pollution. On board, have a look for yourself,
in the ceiling panels at galley centers.

Since deregulation, too, new jets are now configured
without eyeball airvents — the ones above each seat
which provide a personal breeze. I find that this environmental option makes flying much more comfortable.
Usually a lot of air feels good blowing on me at the
beginning and end of flights; overnight, I prefer to close
my vent.

✈ Passengers concerned about personal airflow can carry a
battery-operated, hand-held fan, or they can change seats,
whenever possible, as some rows are airier than others.

✈ If your seat has an airvent which is stuck in the open position, you can cover it with an emergency instruction folder taped across the corners to divert airflow. Ask an attendant to please bring you some tape; there's invariably some in the cockpit.

✈ If a vent is stuck in either the open or closed position, report this to an attendant. Malfunctions will be noted in the Aircraft Maintenance Log, so they will be fixed for the next passenger. (Sadly, though, since deregulation, many maintenance items get deferred.)

Another residual effect of deregulation is the shortage of airline employees at check-in counters. Most probably, this is why passengers are now required to arrive at airports several hours prior takeoff.

✈ When calling reservations, ask at what point prior to scheduled departure one is *required* to check in. Specifically, at what time can you lose your reservation? This varies with routes and carriers. For the record, however, a no-smoking seat on a smoking flight should be legally held until ten minutes prior to departure.

Possibly the airlines could consider incentives for those of us who care to arrive early at airports. Along with greater seat preference, free headsets could be a low-cost carrot to cut down on check-in congestion.

Deregulation has also ushered in the high-density, sardine-like seating on jets — less legroom, less recline, and smaller aisles. I remember exactly when this happened: suddenly my hips were too wide to walk straight down the aisles without bumbing into elbows and shoulders!

Airline management's cost-consciousness for crew has translated into longer duty days, shorter layovers, and short staffing; not to mention crash diets to reduce hips! Crew fatigue is an issue the airlines will need to address soon, I feel, as "airlines still operate on schedules determined by economics, rather than the sleep needs of crew."[91]

For instance, twenty to thirty-hour shifts are common for flight attendants due to scheduling practices and unexpected weather delays.[92] When I worked these flights, we were usually assigned a two-hour rest break en route. This "rest" was taken on a slat stacked in a compartment adjacent to smoking zones, or in a chair visible to passengers, who, and rightly so, never stop asking for things when they see someone in uniform. My dream design uniform has a hat with a light: green for "in service" and red for "on break."

Of course, there's no excuse for a rude airline employee, nor for personal violations that economizing policies foist upon the traveling public. "Violations" is a strong word; I use it to define all *your* airline horror stories — delays without apologies, cramped seats, baggage not showing up or being damaged, smelly aircraft, lack of air-conditioning on the ground during lengthy delays, insufficient food or spoiled food, waiting an unreasonable amount of time in line for a lav, having to wait in line for a lav in the smoking zone when you're a non-smoker, and _____ (fill in the blank) _____.

What to do? Write the airline. Possibly suggest that nice distractions like designer menus or Polaroid photos of passengers at their seats (on some international sectors) or expensive ad campaigns touting so-called award-winning cuisine really don't make up for poor quality air. Do whatever you feel *guided* to do in this regard; anything, that is, except yell at a flight attendant.

Yelling at flight attendants and/or wildly ringing call buttons are common outlets for passenger frustration, leaving attendants caught between a rock and a hard place, between airline marketing ad copy and the reality of short staffing.

For example, before takeoff one day, when I was busy stowing the first-class cabin, the life jacket demo tape began to roll at the same moment a call button rang. Regulations state I have to drop everything and man my demo position beside the video screen. This I did, though simultaneously I acknowledged the call button, first scanning the cabin and then nodding when a male passenger signaled me with a come-hither finger.

A few minutes later, when the demo was over, we were already taxiing. I hurriedly stowed the video screen and picked up a few juice glasses on my way to the gentleman. He looked up at me and said, "I don't feel well," then fell out of his seat face down on the floor. We taxied back to the gate. He left on a stretcher; we heard no more about him.

I felt very angry — at the dehumanizing nature of my job which mandated that it was more important for me to stand by a video screen than to promptly respond to a call button.

When I started flying, we used to run to every button which chimed. One problem today is the location of the buttons. The old ones were overhead, next to the reading lights; now, they are in the armrests. On every flight today, dozens are simply mistaken for the recline and light buttons or are pushed like game buttons by bored kids. Further, they are now triggered by pushing in, instead of pulling out the way they used to, so many are inadvertently set off by elbows. In addition, passengers, especially foreigners, mistake the ones in the lavs for flush buttons.

What's worse, marketing promotes the idea that anyone can have a personal attendant at the push of a button, like an invalid in a hospital. Of course, marketing also crows on-time service, even though planes are late up to 50% of the time.[93]

The era of flight attendants having the time to leap to every call button disappeared with deregulation, too. In this age, the secret for getting whatever you want from busy flight attendants is this: 1) preface your requests with, *When you have time…* and, 2) specifically at meal service, when your attendant asks you what entree you would like, say, *Whatever you have the most of…* or, *No, thank you, I don't care to eat.*

The rising wave of public concern for health and the environment should soon put a stop to the airlines' practice of recycling such a large percent of the air on commercial jets. Instead of recycled air, how about recyling cans from beverage services and pans from meal services? Every three months, Americans throw away enough aluminum to build every jet of U.S. commercial carriers.[94]

Some airlines have now haphazardly instituted aluminum recycling, but only on long-hauls as an option when the crew has time. Without extra staffing and redesigning of service carts, recycling cannot be fully implemented. Perhaps passengers would like to participate — in flight, they could bring their own trays back to an onboard recycling center. They could drop empty sugar packets, for example, in the paper trash and full ones in the "unused supplies." Would passengers object to keeping their drink glasses for the duration of their flights — if they knew it would save an endangered species or two?

Furthermore, instead of using disposable plastic glasses in economy, how about using real glass, like in first and business classes? And what about recycling wine bottles, empty miniatures, newspapers, magazines, time-tables, paper napkins, headrest covers, and milk cartons?

I can see it all now! As aircraft pull into gates around the world, there — instead of idling, diesel-polluting catering-, fuel-, and tow-trucks — are bright, shiny servicing tunnels where wastes are automatically sent to underground recycling centers and where fuel, air, water, and food are efficiently, semi-robotically resupplied.

Airlines are the jet-age bridges of our global sphere. Wouldn't this be an Earth-saving way to spread recycling everywhere? And yet there would still be the larger ecological problem of jet-engine emissions, which contribute to smog and acid rain and deleteriously deplete the ozone layer. Airlines need our encouragement to move towards alternative fuels and fuel-efficient engines — to show that we are one in action.

AGE BEFORE DUTY (Aging Fleet)

The worst airplane accident in aviation history — declared worst because it claimed the most lives, over five hundred (8/85) — has been attributed to something which is called, in aeronautics, "metal fatigue."

A couple of years later (4/88), one-third of another jet's upper fuselage simply peeled away on a flight between Honolulu and Maui, leaving passengers exposed to the elements at 24,000 feet. Only one person lost her life on that flight— a flight attendant just vanished into the sky as she was handing a drink to a passenger. What an abrupt and unfortunate ending to a twenty-year career!

Like its attendant, the aircraft had been flying about twenty years. According to airline analysts, the "economic life" of a jet is about twenty years, though aircraft age is determined more precisely by takeoff/landing cycles. Each cycle includes one pressurization and one depressurization. It's something like when a person puts on a lot of weight then takes it off, rapidly and repeatedly; the skin eventually loses elasticity, as evidenced by stretch marks.

The aircraft which made that emergency landing on Maui was one of the "oldest" jets worldwide, with 89,681 takeoff/landing cycles.[95] One month after that tragedy (5/88), however, another jet made an unscheduled landing at Detroit because a fifteen-inch fuselage crack caused a drop in pressure. A few months after that (10/88), passengers between Rochester and Atlanta reported being able to "see the sky" through a fourteen-inch crack of a twenty-two-year old jet. But it wasn't until nine passengers were sucked out of a 747 in mid air (2/89) that the fuselage-crack crackdown was officially ushered in.

Safety experts debate the limits of older jets and ways to accurately detect cracks. Maintenance crews used to look for the small, dark nicotine stains on aircraft exteriors, caused by cigarette smoke which seeped out of pressurized jets! Uh-oh. Now that there's a smoking ban on many sectors, maintenance has had to get technical. Some airlines use X-ray, ultrasonic probes, dyes, or magneto-optic imaging. Other carriers buff out their fuselages instead of painting them, reasoning that cracks can hide under layers of thick exterior paint. Hawaiian Airlines says that they now repair planes during the day, rather than during overnight stops, as they used to. JAL says they now rotate aircraft between long-range and short-range, to evenly distribute takeoff/landing cycles.

The world's aging fleet is expensive. Older 737s require, for example, eighty new nozzles at about $5,000 each[96] and 7,200 new rivets.[97] The FAA estimates that needed modifications to older 707s will cost a cool $1 million each. There are over four hundred of these jets flying around the world today.[98] Within the next few years, when these regulations go into effect, many older jets will simply be cannibalized for spare parts, experts say. For now, however, pulling planes out of service is not considered economically viable.

Here's a suggestion for the aging-fleet controversy. Jets over ten years old can offer a 25% discount to passengers. Jets over twenty can offer a 90% discount, for the real gamblers! We, the flying public, can collectively demand first-rate equipment for full-fare tickets!

✈ If you feel that your jet is in poor condition, report it to the Aviation Safety Institute, Box 304, Worthington, Ohio 43085 (614/885-4242). Include flight number, date, sector flown, and aircraft number (usually outside and inside the forward left entry door). They would also like to hear from the public regarding aviation accidents.

Fuselage cracks have now alerted the public to the state of the aviation industry. *Crack! Wake up!* they say. Move into new levels of awareness of travel, into travel consciousness — for example, by providing open information on aircraft age, solar flares, ozone wisps, and bomb threats.

HUB RUB (Transit Stops)

Contrary to classical geometry where *the shortest distance between two points is a straight line*, many airlines now practice Hub and Spoke geometry: to get from point A to point B, passengers are required to transit point C.

Of course, nonstops are preferable to playing musical chairs at hubs. However, on many routes today one-stop service (not the "one stop" you want) is the only kind available, as this is most economical for the airlines.

For passengers, hub inconveniences are clear. They mean longer elapsed time on travel days. Also, as most of us know from childhood with musical chairs, something is always left out when the music stops! (Checked luggage? 8% of passengers who checked luggage report them lost or damaged.[99] Maybe this is why 37% of frequent fly-ers indicate they "almost never" check luggage.[100])

Additionally, transit stops require two takeoffs and landings as opposed to only one of each — opening the possibility for double possible trouble, as most problems occur during takeoffs and landings.

Opening the hub gate is like opening a flood gate: instead of nice, steady streams of passengers meander-ing genteelly through airports, hubs cause ebbs and flows which congest gateside restaurants, shops, and airline clubs.

Besides, there's the dreaded domino effect: usually all simultaneous connections are held for one delayed plane. Everyone is compelled to wait until all flights from outlying spokes have arrived and received service at hubs.

✈ A late aircraft arrival is different from a *rolling delay*, which describes a departure that gets pushed back, and back, due to a mechanical problem. In a rolling delay, "you might be better off trying to arrange another flight, as long as you don't have to pay a cancellation penalty or higher fare for changing your reservations."[101]

The most annoying things about flying are the delays, according to 49.6% of frequent flyers surveyed.[102]

✈ To avoid delays, try not to fly during peak periods: 7 - 9 a.m., 4 - 7 p.m.

Many passengers unintentionally end up transiting hubs, misled by the curious airline phrase, *direct flight*.

✈ A direct flight does not necessarily go directly, as it implies; that's a *nonstop*. A direct flight can pick up/drop off passengers at any number of transits along the way, and this often requires deplaning.

✈ A direct flight does not include an aircraft change, however; that's a *connecting flight*.

✈ A *through flight* involves not only an aircraft change,

but an airline change as well.

Some airlines market domestic feeders with international partners, calling them one-stop connections. Passengers get miffed because, in fact, when changing airlines, they are compelled to make time-consuming luggage-*schlepping* terminal shifts. In Los Angeles, for example, transiting passengers from abroad are advised to allow three hours, due to customs' backups and the circuitous path between terminals.

✈ When calling reservations, ask: *Does my routing include a transit stop?* If it does, ask: *Will there be an aircraft change?* If the flight numbers change, the aircraft probably changes. If the letters before the numbers change, too, you've probably got a terminal change.

✈ If you miss your connecting or through flight and it's the airline's fault, they will most likely assume responsibility — i.e., provide hotel and/or get you out on the next available — only if your entire trip is written on one ticket. Weather is the exception; this is not considered airline responsibility.

Otherwise, you may not be able to get a reservation out for hours — or even days during peak periods — and you may not be able to retrieve your checked luggage!

✈ When making reservations, do not book tight connections. (Legal time varies from twenty minutes to a couple of hours, depending on airport and carrier.) This will save you stress with the minor, frequent delays which all carriers encounter.

Some people go to the trouble to book illegal connections under two names because they feel transits are a waste of time. *Au contraire*.

✈ Transits are an excellent place to recoup energy on long-distance trips. Remember: breathing and aerobic walking cuts down on jetlag. Try speed walking around the lounge for twenty minutes, then doing some stretches. Or, consider walking around to the rhythm of your own pulse.

✈ On the bright side, when we jet in hops (up, down, up, down), instead of nonstop, we avoid higher-flying exposures to radiation and ozone. Furthermore, flights with transit stops aren't as dry; the aircraft picks up humidity each time it touches back on Earth. It's really a trade off. A New York to Tokyo nonstop takes almost fourteen hours; with a transit stop in Anchorage, it's about three hours extra.

In the future, hopefully, airport designers will put the "lounge" back in transit lounges. Sleepy transit passengers, now required to disembark, find in the lounge nothing but those oddly designed seats with fixed armrests and a full set of fluorescent lights on high. What to do? I just lie down on the floor when I'm tired, or I go off exploring.

For the undaunted, every airport is a treasure hunt. Seek and ye shall find: rooms for hire by the hour with bed and shower, restaurants featuring local food and vibes, health clubs, office centers, chapels, art galleries, and boutiques.

In Frankfurt and Narita terminals the best shops are outside the transit areas. Without luggage, you can clear immigration and customs in a matter of minutes. Tell customs: *I am in transit.* Show your boarding pass. Be sure to take your passport and ticket, too, and be apprised of local time, and your gate number. Check the monitors periodically for possible gate change. In some airports — Hong Kong's Kai Tak, for example — departure gates are different from arrival ones, even on a different level of the airport.

Ah, shopping…we flight attendants used to run off the plane at transit stops just to shop: salad bowls in Montego Bay, gems in Rio de Janeiro, underwear in

Paris, silver in Sri Lanka, shells in Samoa, Eskimo dolls in Anchorage....

✈ If serenity is your spring, source the meditative air in airport chapels. They are excellent places to take out your internal camera and view some films of yourself arriving safe and happy at your destination locale.

Honolulu airport has a gazebo in the middle of a carp pond — a choice spot for meditating. Use the staircase behind the coffee shop to the lower level of the airport. Clap your hands at the edge of the pond and carp come, kissing the air in expectation of food.

Climate is always something to sample when moving from place to place. One winter, transiting JFK from/to the tropics, I cleared security and adventured out into the snow.

Some airports are only fifteen minutes from a town, while others take hours to negotiate traffic. Check it out with a local: *If you had three hours to spare what would you do here?* Airline employees are usually open to chat when not surrounded by a crowd. Query the ones stationed at that airport, not crews in transit. Or, ask airport Information. Maybe you'd prefer to call a nearby airport hotel and query the concierge. Maybe you'd like to take the hotel courtesy car and use their swimming pool for an hour.

If you find yourself with five hours in NRT (Narita, Japan), for example, taxi to the Narita View Hotel, leave your luggage with the porter, then go down to the health club or follow the path behind the hotel. Meander through a magical wooded area with flowering shrubs and yellow-striped spiders as big as Kennedy half-dollars. Or treat yourself to lunch at the posh European restaurant on the top floor; the view is the best in all of Narita — rice paddies with their long green sprouts undulating in miles of wind.

You never know what you'll discover on a transit stop. I am personally very fond of them, starting with an old transit memory. Before the nonstops from Honolulu to Sydney were inaugurated, we used to transit Pago Pago for about an hour. The island folk met every flight and serenaded us while we refueled and resupplied.

Passengers were always greeted by a local choir in Pago. Natives of all ages — the huge men in shirts and ties with wrap-around skirts; the voluptuous women draped in floral-patterned tunics, children in their arms; teenagers and toddlers — the whole community turned out. They sang their hearts out for about an hour — from 3 to 4 a.m. — then waved us good-bye.

Dragon Wisdom

I experience the creativity and affluence of the Divine Design as It manifests around me and through me.

WHO ARE THE REAL PESTS?

KILLER MIST (Pesticide)

Today's international passengers disembarking in New Zealand will be treated to a shower of pesticide before they are permitted to put even one toe on solid ground. With seatbelts fastened, air-conditioning deactivated, and aircraft doors sealed, pesticide inhalation is a mandatory requirement.

The U.S. ambassador to New Zealand (under Reagan) was returning to duty one night on my flight, and I personally petitioned him. Actually, I begged him to use his influence to put a stop to this practice, as I was regularly flying Aucklands. Still today, though, local authorities fumigate all arriving planeloads for what they call a "fifteen-minute saturation period." Day after day, passengers and crew are gassed with this so-called "vital barrier against the introduction of a number of vectors of serious human, plant, and animal diseases."[103]

Pesticide saturates clothes and hair and soaks into skin, so it's really a matter of hours before we're pesticide-free: after customs, after the bus ride to hotel, after check-in, after shampoo, after laundering clothes in hot water.

✈ There is a way to disembark prior to the pesticide spray:

Step One. Ask your doctor to write you a note saying you are allergic to pesticides, asthmatic, or pregnant.

Step Two. Mention your "allergy" to the purser on descent; inquire which exit will be used for disembarkation. Wonder aloud, *Hmm, would it expedite matters for me to be re-seated near the exit for landing?* in case s/he doesn't suggest this first.

Step Three. After touchdown, get up and move towards the designated exit with all your personal effects — yes, on taxi. Otherwise, you won't get out in time. Authorities, usually three men with two cans of pesticide each, quickly board. You've got to slip out (with their permission, of course) after you show your note but before they start their ritual.

A representative from the New Zealand Ministry of Agriculture explained to me that the pesticide is not harmful to humans, that it has, in fact, been approved by the World Health Organization. He claimed the pesticide is not even designed to kill pests, only stun them, in the quaint hope that all stunned bugs will disembark from everyone before we disembark the aircraft. What about those stunned bugs which fall inert into pant cuffs only to wake up refreshed in a closet at the Auckland Sheraton?

Having been sprayed over a hundred times, I can attest that the cumulative effect definitely stuns humans. The toxic shower caused my eyes to drip yellow pus within twelve hours of spraying. I also suffered, routinely, a loss of motor coordination, making me trip over my own feet and sometimes fall down, within thirty minutes of exposure.

Then, on the very week of my 21st anniversary as a

flight attendant, I contracted a severe case of the flu and was grounded. The weeks drew out to months, then years. Now I'm permanently "medically grounded" due to what is called, environmental sensitivity. You know how kryptonite affects Superman? That's how petro-chemical derivatives affect me. I now have to avoid dry-cleaned clothes, carpets, newsprint, plastics, paint, propane, even perfumes. My doctor clearly attributes this "acute sensitivity" to pesticide exposure.

For the passenger being sprayed, the problem is compounded by increased susceptibility to physical and chemical insults after long hours of breathing recycled air (eight from Hawaii, fifteen from California). Not only that, passengers are all the more vulnerable to gassing after sleep deprivation. Most Down Under-bound aircraft are red-eyes.

Bug enthusiasts could try this pesticide experiment at home. Catch some insects and divide them into two jars. Keep one group up all night, and let the others sleep. In the morning, spray both groups with pesticide — and watch which ones kick over first!

Experiments like this are performed today, every flight, between Bangkok and Delhi, too, and from anywhere to Australia. Flight attendants are required to empty half a dozen cans of pesticide into the passengers' air supply en route, then hand over the proof to local authorities: twelve empty cans of pesticide (six discharged prior to departure). "What could they be trying to prevent from entering India?" passengers ask over and over in toxic bewilderment.

Additionally, the U.S. Department of Agriculture fumigates planes on some domestic flights prior to take-off, when there are regional proliferations of beetles. On many international sectors, too, airlines regularly "paint" their cargo holds with pesticide. The contents

of our checked luggage get contaminated; porous soft
luggage is more likely a problem than hard cases.

✈ After landing, clean luggage before carrying into bedroom, and especially before placing on bed to unpack.

As aircraft transit the world, pesticide residue lingers,
endangering the well-being of passengers and crew.
Today's passengers are not even forewarned when they
make reservations. There is, prior to spray, simply a glib
announcement, "The slight discomfort you may feel...."
These same announcements were used until 1972 when
DDT was the pesticide of choice. Now a pyrethrin is used.

✈ Join the worldwide wave protesting pesticide spray.
Public outcry is our greatest repellent force against
countries who still use these volatile bug bombs.

LOVE CANAL VS JET STREAM (Toxic Chemicals)
It is common knowledge today that many industrial
practices have polluted our global environment. "The
dangers of exposure to toxic substances are greater than
people realize," says the National Environmental Law
Center.[104]

We may not even be aware of the fact that many
products we use in our personal lives are serious pol-
luters. Everyday articles which most of us do not even
consider contaminants can be provocateurs to the sensitive. Among these are most cleaning compounds, adhe-
sives, and printers' ink. (Non-polluting, soy-based ink
was used to print the text and cover of this book.)

On jets, in the enclosed cabin with its compromised
air, the finish on furnishings (seats and carpets) and the
plastic materials used in bulkheads are also a source of
toxicity to passengers and crew. Fabrics contain
formaldehyde and other toxic chemicals to render them
fresh-looking. And, new plastics actually *out-gas* poi-
sonous fumes. "If one could see the molecular activity

on the surface of an active material, such as some plastics and paints, it would appear to be slowly boiling, releasing a cloud of gas into the surrounding air," writes William Rea, M.D.,[105] a cardiovascular surgeon specializing in environmental medicine.

Additionally, passengers are subjected to toxic chemical fumes from fuel exhaust, especially prior to takeoff, when wind can funnel a jet's own exhaust or that of a maintenance vehicle passing nearby right back into cabin air. Idling on runways, engines are less efficient and emit higher concentrations of carbon monoxide, oxides of nitrogen, hydrocarbons, aldehydes, and polynuclear aromatic compounds,[106] inundating aircraft cabins with contaminated air.[107] People seated in taxiing planes may notice a strong diesel-fuel smell prior to takeoff.

Another potential source of toxic fumes is the cargo hold. Shipments of hazardous stuff are regularly transported aboard commercial jets and noxious fumes enter the passengers' air supply when they topple or leak.[108] Vials of viruses and germs also crisscross the world as airline cargo.[109]

A final source of toxic fumes on jets is fire — after a jet crash, passengers who survive the impact are sometimes asphyxiated en route to exits. A case in point is the runway collision in Detroit (12/90) where, according to the report, all fatalities were caused by "noxious fumes." Some of the toxic gases that form when an airplane combusts include: cyanide, chlorine, and carbon monoxide.[110]

✈ There are protective, closed-circuit breathing devices available.[111] This FAA certified technology is now installed on aircraft for crew to use for in-flight fires, and ought to be made available to passengers, to help people survive post-crash fires.

ENGLISH MUFFIN (EM Pollution)

A recent issue of global controversy centers on the invisible energy of electromagnetic (EM) fields. Like the charismatic actor of old, W.C. Fields, EM fields have their own unique electric charge and magnetic attraction. In the latter, however, the attraction is believed to be fatal, including reports of cancer and miscarriages,[112] due to the depression of the immune system.[113]

When I became chemically sensitive in 1987, I found I had also acquired a heightened feel for EM fields. For me, these are real health hazards causing signals of headache, fever, lightheadedness, and — what was it, it will come to me, oh, yes — short-term cognitive memory loss.

I first became aware of this *energy* when I lived within a few miles of a military base which used a radar surveillance system; whenever I drove within its range, I promptly became ill. Acute sensitivity like mine is unusual, but not unheard of. "Electromagnetic sensitivity exists as a definite clinical entity," explains environmental expert, Dr. Rea.[114]

What helps to keep me functional in the world's highly-charged environment is to wear an elemental diode — a light-weight, copper-colored, unassuming, inch-and-a-half square tile which easily slips into pockets and underwear. "The diode enhances the aura surrounding the body," writes visionary Wayne Cook,[115] who spent thirty-two years researching things like biomagnetic and psychoenergetic force fields.

✦ The diode, worn beneath the clothing evokes a definite rise in well-being by dispelling invisible EM charges.

In 1989, *Sharper Image Catalog* featured a diode pad, which they suggested that airline passengers sit on in order to offset jetlag. They discontinued it the following year. I think it didn't sell well because the model they promoted was too bulky for travel; the smaller ones are more convenient and fully adequate. In addition, the advantage of diodes is not necessarily for jetlag, rather for the jet-snag EM pulses encountered at airports and on jets.

EM activity is most dense in the vicinity of international airports with microwave landing systems, and less dense in airports where they only have microwave fast-food ovens!

On jets, EM pollution is believed to be caused by ground and airborne radar for weather and air traffic, cockpit computers, jet engines, and electrical wiring throughout an aircraft's fuselage. At this time, there is no information available on the sources and/or effects of EM pulsations in commercial airline cabins.

There has been substantial research, however, into the various sources of EM pollution closer to the ground, affording us a lot of reasons to feel frazzled in everyday life! EM pulses emanate whenever there is electricity, most notably from fluorescent lights, dimmer switches, electric blankets, electrically-heated water beds, t.v.s, microwave ovens, copy machines, computers, X-rays, radar, power lines, hair dryers, blenders, refrigerators, elevators — all the electric smog of our high-tech life. "Some European governments have standards which restrict exposures of their workers to levels which are one thousand times less than ours."[116] The Office of Technology Assessment recommends "prudent avoidance."[117]

Today, aviation engineers admit that menstrual cycles of flight attendants are probably affected by EM fields in jets; it's the iron content in blood, they suspect, which is pulled towards the fields, then clumps, as iron filings do. Until such time as adequate standards and safeguards are established for EM exposures in jets, it appears unfair for flight attendants and passengers to be governed by obsolete exposure guidelines such as the English muffin standard: "the implication that microwave radiation was harmless as long as you didn't turn brown or feel toasty."[118]

All flyers will be well-served when research in the cabin environment gives evidence of sources, sites, and incidence of significant exposures.

It is well known that EM pulses can be used to affect behavior. Electro-shock therapy is one application. Another, in the sixties, was concocted by the Soviets, who regularly "stimulated" the U.S. Moscow Embassy and succeeded in modifying the behavior of those who worked there.[119]

It's possible that the airlines' disregard for the effects of EM fields on commercial aircraft has resulted in behavioral problems among crew and passengers.

✦ To help ameliorate the effects of both non-ionizing radiation (EM fields) as well as ionizing (cosmic) radiation, drink a lot of water to flush, lubricate, and vitalize the body's own electrical charge; take baking soda/sea salt baths after landing to draw out toxins through the pores; and eat chlorophyll-rich greens, (spinach, seaweed, etc.).[120]

PUFF THE TRAGIC DRAG (Tobacco Smoke)
Unable to smoke aboard a one-hour Southwest flight, passenger Charles Compton was so upset he handed the crew a note claiming he had explosives and was going to hijack the plane to Cuba![121] (Compton was purportedly the reincarnation of Sir Walter Raleigh, the courtier of Elizabeth I, who first introduced the uncivilized habit of smoking to the civilized world.) Things having come full circle; Compton was jailed, not knighted, for this tobacco-related incident. Call it karma, if you will!

As I'm sure Compton would agree, the inflight envi-

ronment does, indeed, create a special state of withdrawal for the addicted; in this context, the FAA has ruled to
allow cigarette-smoking pilots, stating that possible
withdrawal symptoms "are associated with decrements in
vigilance, in concentration, and with increased agita-
tion, anxiety, and aggression."[122] By the way, second-
hand smoke exhaled from pilots does not filter into the
passenger cabins; air-circulation is separate.

Passengers experiencing nicotine withdrawals often
resort to arguments with flight attendants. Some light up
at their seats anyway. Others try to deactivate a lav smoke
detector by placing a shower cap or condom over it.

✈ Anyone who "tampers with an airline smoke alarm"
can be charged with a federal offense and fined $2000.

In fact, multiple fines are applied to those with the
temerity to light up where prohibited. For example,
"smoking in a lav" is another fine of $1000, and "smok-
ing when a no-smoking sign is illuminated" is still
another $1000.

So far, Air Canada is the only airline to innovate a
smoking ban on all passenger aircraft, with the exception of its London-Bombay route.

The toxic exhalations from smokers on commercial
jets permeate all cabins on board, obviously, when half
of aircraft air is recirculated. Non-smokers can complain
from here to Bombay, there is no way airlines can deliv-
er uncontaminated air — anywhere — when smokers
are on board.

On commercial jets "there is no significant difference in exposure between the smoking and no-smoking
areas,"[123] reports a study done by the National Cancer
Institute. Not only that, the jet environment renders
this unwanted nicotine all the more toxic, because
cigarette smoke coupled with high-altitude air is
known to inactivate a person's hemoglobin, producing

temporary anemia.[124]

Yet, as we travel around the world, we still meet with pockets of diehard smokers who are inflexible in their determination to cloud the air. "On a trip a few weeks ago, I pointed my air jet over my head to force back the smoke of the passenger behind me," a subscriber wrote to *Frequent Flyer*. "He actually argued I was being unfair to him! He felt his right to smoke was more reasonable than my right to direct the air jet. I had fun with him!"[125]

The domestic smoking ban in the United States is only the first step towards global consciousness of this issue. Over most parts of the world today, inflight air reeks of burnt nicotine. Even Lufthansa, the meticulous German carrier, was unable to institute a no-smoking policy on domestic sectors due to passengers' protests.[126]

On flights to and from Japan, where passengers puff like choo-choo trains from takeoff till landing, clouds of smoke are so thick that the alarms in the lavs spontaneously *brrrring* even with no one smoking in them.

International airlines are beginning to note that many flight attendants are staying clear of smoking zones; as a result, those passengers complain of feeling "neglected." Cabin crews, however, are beginning to voice their own complaints. All over the world, attendants are suing airlines for negligence in providing a healthy work environment. A recent $5 billion product liability class-action case was brought by flight attendants against nine tobacco companies.

Doctors say the particulate matter from cigarette smoke is responsible for allergic rhinitis — the runny nose and sneezing some passengers suffer while traveling on board flights where smoking is permitted.

Aircraft manufacturers say that there is no way to increase ventilation levels without completely redesign-

ing aircraft ventilation systems. Added to this, some airlines allow smokers to stand up at the back of the aircraft and/or around galley centers, creating a thick cur-
tain of murk.

✈Most airlines locate their smoking section at the aft of
aircraft because the outflow valves are around the last
row of each cabin. On the DC-10-10, however, the outflow valves are at the front, so the smoking section, on
United at least, is forward of the non-smoking one.

Certainly the airlines would benefit from a total
smoking ban: ventilation filters and cabin interiors
would require less cleaning, seat selection at check-in
would be simplified, and the risk of inflight fires would
diminish.

✈ To appease both camps, the airlines might at least
install ionizers to draw smoke and other pollutants out
of the air; any airline which takes this initiative would
certainly receive passenger recognition as a forerunner
of the new hygienic and holistic outlook of our time.

✈ In smoke-filled planes, to help alleviate irritation,
breathe through a water-soaked hanky and keep eyes
closed and/or covered with an eye-mask.

✈ Although there is a tendency to stop breathing near
cigarette smoke, it is important to practice conscious
breathing. Inhale/exhale to a balanced set count which
you choose. Feel the air flow in/out as you do.

Dragon Wisdom

I relax in rarefied atmosphere high above the clouds.
Only Exquisite Energy distills to me from this air. I
thrive on the quality of air I breathe.

THE SOUNDS OF PROGRESS

SAY WHAT? (Noise)

She must be deaf, I heard a passenger say about me one flight — intending for me to overhear because I had forgotten to bring him something. Hearing loss, nonetheless, is common among crew, from the dual chronic stressors of rapid barometric change and noisy planes.

Audible levels inside jets, especially in galleys, can reach up to 96 decibels, high enough to cause permanent impairment when sustained for long periods of time.[127] My hearing disability, and that of another attendant I know, involves the simultaneous juxtaposition of two sounds, and requires that one has a steady hum, like a vacuum cleaner.

On flights, this *sshhhmmmm* is caused by the jet engines, the friction of the plane with the outside air, and the cabin air-conditioning system. The combination can be quite numbing to the brain. In fact, only one positive thing can be said about noise levels in jets; they muffle all small sounds, making the cabin a farter's haven!

Since the advent of jets, a tremendous amount of

research has been focused on noise pollution, starting with the *brouhaha* of residents neighboring airports who protest against the loud, recurrent engine peals and whines on takeoffs and landings. "Noise is where cigarette smoking was 30 years ago. Everybody knows it's bad for you, but a lot of people don't do anything about it."[128]

Residents of Newark, New Jersey, are complaining, however. Their tesitomy to the FAA states that aircraft noise near a school is so severe it disrupts classes thirteen times per hour.[129] Another skirmish in the war against airport noise has resulted in an award of $124 million for impaired hearing to neighbors of a military base in Japan.[130]

On a more positive note, the environment-friendly new Munich II Airport is now paying to soundproof thousands of private homes near the airport, as well as charging up to 50% higher landing fees for older, louder planes.[131]

The effect of noise pollution on people is *level dependent* — i.e., our problems are contingent upon the level of noise, both in regards to peak episodes and sustained sounds. In addition to hearing impairment, scientists now associate mental hospital admissions (29% increase) with airport proximity.[132]

In 1985, the FAA enforced a ban on the noisy, first-generation passenger jets, the 707s and DC-8s. The remaining noisy aircraft must be modified or retired as follows: 55% by 1994, 65% by 1996, 75% by 1998, and 100% by 2000. Some local airports want noise reductions even sooner. But airlines are pushing for what they call scheduling conformity,[133] i.e., without the same regulations at all airports, they say, they cannot operate effectively.

For passengers, auditory disorientation starts at the

embarkation airport, peaks on board, and continues until we close the door to a hotel room or private residence after landing. The mechanized air at airports and on flights can affect our ears the way a flashing light grabs the attention of our eyes. And the combined sounds when flying — humming, babbling, blaring, roaring, pealing, ringing, whooshing, purring, whining, and thudding — can dazzle the brain into a peculiar stupor.

Airline employees who work the tarmacs wear ear muffs.

✦ Passengers can also cut down on noise-related stressors by investing in ear plugs. The plugs will be inconvenient at airports where we need to hear announcements. But, once on board, consider plugging up.

✦ The type of ear plugs I prefer are made from foam and conform to the shape of the ear. Plain sterile cotton works well, too, to muffle rather than block sound altogether. This is *safe* for flight, in the sense we can still hear if loud emergency instructions are initiated.

✦ When making reservations, consider choosing flights on jets known to be quieter, such as the Fokker 100.

✦ Another approach to the obstreperous problem of jet noise is to listen to headphones while on board.

✦ A subtle-energy approach to inflight noise is to fling oneself headlong into the various sounds. While sitting comfortably in your seat take time out to isolate these sounds — the engine *mmmm*, the *sshhh* as the aircraft speeds through space, the *whoosh* of the cabin air-conditioning system, voices over the PA, other passengers conversing, foreign languages spoken, even a baby crying. Feel safe knowing the origins of all these sounds. Listen to the subtle rhythms, too. What is the tune of this language? Rise above the din. Experience the cacophony as an orchestra tuning up; pick out the various instruments. Do the strings tie you to someone or somewhere?

✈After landing, listen to the obvious sounds of town as well as the unheard sounds around. Take time to tune into the combined rhythms of the local social cycle. Notice the tone the cars honk, the speed the elevators rise, and the pace the people stride.

NO POP (Aerotitis)

As aircraft descend, pressure increases, and this usually causes ear drums to vibrate the sound *pop*. When descent is a pain in the ear, it's called aerotitis or blocked ear — an excruciating signal experienced by those who fly with a cold or an ear infection.

✈To adjust your ears on descent, yawn, swallow or raise and harden (from inside) the back of your tongue.

✈Occasionally these measures are too subtle. If so, try the valsalva maneuver: hold your nostrils and mouth closed and gently blow out.

✈Or, adjust your ears with steam-heat:

Step One. Place two airline paper cocktail napkins in the bottom of a small wax-coated drinking cup, the ones found at the lav and galley drinking water dispensers. Add boiling water from a galley hot-water spigot, to cover. CAUTION: Be sure to drain off ALL excess water.

Step Two. Cover the blocked ear with the cup of damp tissue. Pain eases in moments as steam clears the eustachian tube.

✈To adjust infants' ears on ascent/descent, offer them something to suck and swallow.

✈On board, if you ever experience ear pain, communicate this to an attendant. Request that the pilot be informed. Pilots have told me that they can repressurize manually, affording more subtle adjustments than by computer. At the very least, the incident will be registered in the ship's log, so aircraft repressurization valves will be checked by a maintenance crew after landing.

Some passengers prefer to take a decongestant to pre-vent blocked ears. Decongestants have side-effects, however, such as dry mouth and drowsiness, which exacerbate jetlag.

Along with ear pain, signals of aerotitis can also include temporary hearing loss, vertigo, amplification of one's own voice, and tinnitus — ringing, whistling, hissing and roaring sounds in the ear. For some passen-gers, symptoms only begin to manifest a couple of days after landing.

Dragon Wisdom

I tune into changes in sound and pressure as aspects of the Grand Composer. I ensure that the hums and haws which I caw are nourishing for others.

E.MEERWALD   J.P. WCZYK

DEUTSCHES REICH

SIGNS OF THE TIMES

18 SECONDS (Emergency)

When Pan Am's flight #103 blew out of the sky over Lockerbie, Scotland (12/88), "Terrorism!" was the mourning cry for the dead. Due to terrorists' threats, travelers worldwide now submit to body checks and X-rayed personal effects.

However, by the time most of us have reached these security bottlenecks, we've stopped thinking about hijackers and are contemplating, instead, the contents of our own handcarries — especially those of us carrying diskettes or film. Yes, Kodak's high-speed film is now marked "protect from X-ray," and scrambled data has been reported by flyers. Even medications, such as insulin, are known to lose potency from these X-rays. No one knows for sure why: it may be a knob turned too high, a security agent's too-lingering eye, or simply a cumulative effect of too many rays.

Some passengers now buy those iron-plated pouches to carry their medications, film, and data. I prefer to avoid this extra weight in my carry-on, so I ask for hand inspection.

✈ Say to security, *I know the X-ray is not supposed to ruin my film* (or disks, or medication), *but would you please do a visual check for me, anyway? I just can't take a chance today with this.*

✈ To help prevent quarrels with security personnel, arrive early and take time to offer a smile.

✈ When clearing security anywhere in the world, always keep an eye on your own personal effects.

✈ Don't even whisper the words "hold up," "hijack" or "bomb" near security, on a jet, or even in the vicinity of an airport. On 2/91 a passenger who said, "I have a bomb. Only kidding," was fined $28,000.[134]

Yet, in spite of all this expense to waylay terrorists with guards and high-tech gadgets, security experts overtly agree: the world's airports are far from airtight!

A case in point is the exploit of a grieving parent of a Lockerbie victim who carried a pretend-bomb through Heathrow,[135] #103's last transit before Lockerbie. Another example was the Israeli security ace who smuggled dummy explosives through six European airports, undetected.[136]

What invariably does get detected, however, are the pocket knives or knitting needles of non-terrorists like you and me. Items are then tagged for baggage claim, causing tedious delay later, as they are usually too small for the carousel ride and require hand pick-up at Lost and Found.

On board, prior to takeoff, we pick up the thread of aviation emergency with the introduction of the flight-attendant demonstration which familiarizes passengers with life jackets, rafts, and escape procedures. These demos are definitely cloaked in euphemism, avoiding some important information. Here are two examples: 1) in the event of a fire, polyester clothing will melt into a person's skin; 2) during a chute escape, pantyhose will cause raspberry burns on legs and fannies.

In fact, demos are usually such boring rituals that nobody watches. Passenger inattentiveness was even cited by the National Transportation Safety Board as a major crash survival problem. For example, at a Malaga crash (10/82), fifty people died in an aft cabin despite usable exits at the forward end of the plane.[137]

✈Smart-class passengers watch demos and review emergency instruction folders.

Nowadays, on most airlines, live demos have been replaced by unimaginative videos. Too bad people aren't inspired to watch. In the event of a rapid decompression we have only "18 seconds of useful consciousness" in which to pull down an oxygen mask and start breathing. This number is for jets cruising at 40,000 feet, experts say. At 30,000 feet, it's about a minute, because there's a slower rate of decompression. These time periods are, also, of course, relative to the physical stamina of each individual on board.

A rapid decompression is recognized by a loud bang, a rushing of air, a temperature drop, ear aches, and a tornado of carry-ons.[138] Additionally, compartment doors open at each passenger's seat and oxygen masks drop within reach.

✈If you see oxygen masks drop, pull one. This releases a pin in the packing apparatus to start the oxygen flow.

The aircraft master tank contains only enough oxygen to keep everyone on board alive for about ten minutes. However, it is comforting to note that commercial airlines train pilots to complete a dive into what they call an "amicable altitude" in approximately three minutes.

One day, during sudden turbulence between Tokyo and Los Angeles, oxygen compartments accidently opened and masks dropped. In unison, several hundred Japanese passengers pulled masks to their faces and, flawlessly duplicating the earlier demo choreography, turned their heads first to the left, then to the right.

Most Japanese passengers attentively watch demos, even nodding now and again, to show they understand. We should all imitate them. When there's only "18 seconds of useful consciousness," there isn't time to wonder. (By the way, it's not necessary to turn your head to the left and right. Attendants display masks this way so passengers on both sides of the aisles can see.)

Shortly after the demo, passengers are again reminded of emergencies during the pre-departure securing phase. My one and only aborted takeoff convinced me, forever, of the wisdom of these security warnings. That day, as the pilot slammed on the brakes, that which was not secured flew fast forward.

Securing includes stowing carts, compartments, carry-ons, bins, tables, and footrests. Seats must be upright, too, to facilitate access and egress, and seatbelts must be fastened.

Once airborne, jets meet with pitch (nose up, nose down), yaw (nose up to right or left), roll (sideways), climb, sink, and speed differentials. People occasionally get sick from these motions, with symptoms of clammy skin and nausea.

Some passengers use medicated patches for motion sickness. I don't recommend them. The patches need be in place an hour prior to the turbulence; even cockpit computers can't predict this. And, the patches have a side-effect incompatible with jetting in a dry aircraft — dry mouth.

✈ If you need to *toss your cookies*, use an airsick bag found in all seatpockets. After turbulence, dump the entire bag in a toilet.

✈ If you need an extra bag, ask other passengers for theirs.

For safety's sake, it's best for flight attendants to have their seatbelts fastened, too, during periods of turbulence. A co-worker of mine was injured without one; in fact, the damage later required knee surgery.

"The seatbelt sign was off," she related. "Smooth sailing. No warning from the cockpit. Suddenly we hit an updraft like a giant fist came out of the sky and knocked the aircraft nose up. It slammed me into the floor. Both of us working the nose disembarked in wheelchairs. Passengers were all strapped in and they were O.K. One man in a lav managed to hold on but he came out all blue — covered with that blue toilet stuff."

Although airlines request passengers to wear seatbelts "low and tight," as a general rule I believe in slack seatbelts. In the worst situations, such as the explosive decompression of 2/89, no seatbelt is adequate — nine passengers that night, with their seats, flew out the hole in the fuselage.

✈ A slack seatbelt leaves freedom to squirm and this is easier on circulation and back fitness.

✈ Fasten seatbelt outside your blanket on nightflights, so in the event of turbulence while you sleep, attendants will leave you in peace.

Waking people to do up their seatbelts is part of the overall flight attendants' responsibility as mandated by the FAA. Towards this end a highly-technical annual recurrent training has been designed. The review includes familiarity with oxygen use; dry chemical, halon, CO_2, and water-based fire extinguishers; inflatable vests and rafts; and transmitters for rescue.

Even airsick bags, we are taught, can be enlisted as emergency equipment; for example, to use a sonar beacon after crashing in a desert, we are instructed to urinate, neatly, into an airsick bag, then submerge the unit. After fifteen minutes the water-soluble tape dissolves, releasing a whip antenna which then transmits the aircraft's bearing 26 miles omni-directionally, with an operating life of 48 hours.

The annual emergency review also covers hyperventilation, mouth-to-mouth resuscitation, the Heimlich maneuver, cardiac arrest, bleeding, burns, inflight death, food poisoning, hijackers, delivering babies, and evacuating by land or sea.

By land, slide down a chute and flee. By sea, we assemble on the chutes, then unzip from the mothership, and, *voila*, a raft for about fifty folks.

We are reminded to hurry. Why? First, a ditched jumbo jet is predicted to float for only fifty minutes. And, second, "in most serious crashes, 50% of the 10 available exits on 747s fail to work properly."[139]

✈ Prior to takeoff, count the rows between your seat and exits in both directions, in case of heavy smoke from a fire.

This kind of information sometimes makes people afraid to fly. Please read on.

COLD FEET (Fear of Flying)

The gorgeous entertainer Cher boarded my flight one night looking like plain Jane. She quietly took her first-class seat, then clearly indicated: no food, no drink, no conversation. The next time I looked up she was asleep without even having reclined her seat.

The press says Cher's afraid to fly, something millions of us do in relative calm. Mohammed Ali's another one. He's done what most of us could never do — box with big guys. He's afraid to fly, too. "The only thing in the world I'm scared of is flying," I heard him confess on Australian t.v. "I imagine the plane splitting in two, and me falling into the ocean, and then the sharks biting me!"

Every trained athlete knows it is better to relax and

roll with the punches; a tense body will feel an even greater amount of shock. Tension and fear make for a harder bout with jetlag, too. It's too bad Ali couldn't apply his usual positive attitude to travel. If only he said to himself: *I like to fly. I feel at home in the sky.*

Many people reason with themselves that it's safe to fly, but they still feel fear. Sometimes a little mechanical trouble with the safety video prior to takeoff is enough to trigger the darkest sense of foreboding in some passengers. Flight attendants identify these folks as *white-knucklers* — because of the way they grip their armrests. Another signal we watch for is rapid, shallow breathing: hyperventilation.

Incursions (near runway misses) are the latest collective crash worry. U.S. incursions occur approximately 1:13,000 flights. There are twice that many takeoffs every month out of Chicago's O'Hare alone![140]

Another common cause for worry is overwork and understaffing of controllers. During the seven minutes prior to the runway crash at LAX (2/91), the culpable controller had handled fifteen planes!

Weather is always a problem. It's terrifying playing peek-a-boo through fog. And, wind shear (upside-down tornadoes invisible on radar) has caused at least a dozen fatal accidents. Wind rotor (sideways tornadoes), can be fatal, too, killing all on board in Colorado (3/91).

Now that you've read this text, you may have some new aviation fears — possibly radiation and ozone. If you're looking for a reason not to fly, it's easy enough to find one. Even a gremlin on the wing.

What would you guess is the biggest cause of airline emergencies today? *Aviation Week* says it's "human error," causing 66% of all airline accidents.[141] For example, Japan Air Lines wants to indict the four employees at Boeing who improperly repaired their jet. Right after

Boeing serviced it, it crashed (8/85). Boeing excuses its technicians with "human error" and refuses extradition.[142] Possibly a more serious example of human error comes from the annals of the now-bankrupt Eastern Airlines. Over a four-year period mechanics regularly and intentionally installed defective gauges which allowed planes to take off when they weren't safe. They've now been criminally indicted.[143] However, the British Airways mechanic who repaired a windshield with the wrong size bolts, causing a captain to get partially sucked out at 17,000 feet (6/90) was never indicted. The pilot got frostbite; the mechanic got suspension on full pay.[144]

Experts blamed the 12/90 Detroit runway collision on four sets of human errors: 1) the controllers, 2) the airport designers, 3) the manufacturer of the tailcone release device, and 4) the pilots.[145]

Is it human error when a fatigued pilot crashes at a congested airport in bad weather? To err is human. And to be human means one day to face death. Isn't this truth, unconfronted, the source of all this fear of flying?

✈ If you think you are afraid to fly, examine your fear with the magnifying lens of self awareness. Maybe your fear really doesn't belong to you; it could have been inherited from someone else. It could even be religious; until the jet age, after all, the only way to fly was with angels after death!

Or, maybe it isn't fear at all, but real, tangible hypoxia, in which case you need to ask for oxygen on board.

✈ If you think you are afraid to fly, read statistics. "Risk analysts at Lloyds of London have rated flying nearly thirty times safer than driving."[146]

✈ Take responsibility. Admit to yourself, *I am the only one who can do anything about my fear of flying — no travel agent, no airline, no little pill or big machine, not even my mother, can do more for me than I can do for myself.*

✈ Once you've identified the root of your fear, your statistical odds for survival, and your own responsibility, make a cognitive choice to face life (and flying) as the open-ended adventure that it is — choose to fly fearlessly.

Remember the jet that crashed in a cornfield in Sioux City, Iowa (7/89)? First, there was an explosion, then hydraulic failure. 110 people died.

But, 186 survived! This was attributed, in part, to local rescue efforts: two doctors available for every hospitalized patient, residents waiting in line for hours just to donate blood[147] — the whole town responded in moments. Uncannily, two years prior to the accident, this town had actually "run through a drill in which a large plane was assumed to have crashed nearby and 150 survivors needed immediate help."[148]

One survivor told the press: "When you come through something like this, you feel like you have some time you didn't think you would have, so you look at everything as being a little more valuable." Another survivor put it this way: "I'm going to be a lot nicer."[149]

Many people who come through near-death experiences go on to live richer lives. In facing death, they say, the secret of life is revealed.

✈ Employ fear of flying as an opportunity to look at life differently. Be prepared to die. Take a fantasy visualization of your death. *See* your life's end. This is how to die before you fly, to clear fear of flying.

"Ladies and gentlemen," I said to a full first-class cabin one morning, "I have something to tell you." All passengers suddenly grayed. A hijacker? Engine trouble?

I hadn't meant to distress anyone; I was simply in a hurry. So I quickly resumed, "Sorry to startle you; there's nothing to worry about. We have no knives and forks on board, that's what I need to tell you. No cutlery provisioned today. Do you still want us to serve dinner?"

Passengers, at once relieved, visibly began to twitter like baby birds. One woman with a toddler held up a bag of plastic forks, "Will these help?" Applause and cheers. As a result of this camaraderie, the flight ended up to be one of the most pleasant of my career.

Another day, Sammy Davis, Jr., the famous dancer/ singer, boarded at London's Heathrow with smiles and "Hi!"s for everyone, then proceeded to crack jokes for a solid thirteen hours to Los Angeles. Even when we ran short of fuel and made an unscheduled stop in Gander, Newfoundland, he set a friendly tone, standing outside on the snowy tarmac greeting all who approached and signing autographs.

As a smiling flight attendant, I noticed that most passengers were always quite willing to smile back at me. Sometimes they even initiated smiles between us. Rarely, however, will passengers flex their smile muscles at each other. Perhaps this will change when travelers learn that the social cue of familiarity helps to balance our circadian rhythms — i.e., friendly passengers experience less jetlag.[150]

✈ Every flight is an opportunity for each of us to treat fellow travelers as significant others — indeed, to help turn the tide on jetlag worldwide.

Dragon Wisdom

I am much more than my body; my essence travels faster to any place in the world than any plane in the sky.

Taming the Dragon

SEAT OF CIVILIZATION

TACT OR FRICTION (Body Language)
Now you know how the temporary dislocation we experience due to a timezone shift (MEETING THE DRAGON) is compounded by the issues of microbial infection, toxic sprays, cancer-causing radiation, and aircraft blow-outs six miles high (STALKING THE DRAGON). At this point you may choose to say, I don't care if I ever fly again — even with plugs in my ears and oil inside my nose!

Indeed, jetting can be risky, but you can be sure it is not something people will stop doing because of the risks involved. In this sense, jetting is a little like giving birth. And, yes, jets are womb-like capsules which carry us — all crunched up — and then eject us under bright lights. But wombs sustain the well-being of babies, as opposed to the environments of many commercial jets, which drain the well-being of passengers.

Babies can't do anything about their situation. We, however, can — especially collectively. Another similarity between jetting and the birth experience is that

both events are awesome. We tend to feel a little help-
less. This helplessness we experience on flights is but a
prelude to the infantile newness of the foreign place —
where we discover that we can't even read a street sign.

For jet travelers this unusual disorientation is often
referred to as "culture shock" or "culture clash." I call it
jet-tag, in reference to the fact that we have to re-name
or re-tag everything in our new environment. Thus,
even if we follow all the suggestions in this book we will
still experience jet-tag when we fly, and especially when
we go to a land where we don't know the language.

Think of how many maneuvers international travelers have to go through, for example, between an initial
feeling of hunger and the full satisfaction after a good
meal. Some of the most obvious extra steps are: change
money, get the name of a good restaurant, study a city
map, translate a menu, and adjust to unfamiliar foods.
For those of us who get grouchy when hungry, well....

✈ To expedite jet-tag, we need to adjust what we eat
and when we eat, our money attitudes, even our choice
of words, and our *body language*.

Body language is a non-verbal aspect of communica-
tion. For instance, Japanese people generally won't say
"No!" directly. Instead, they gently wave one hand back
and forth in front of their mouths.

In India, by contrast, people slightly raise a chin
when they mean *no*. And they slide their heads right-
left-right when they mean *yes*.

✈ If you are new to the eyes and minds of the people of
your destination land, your best strategy for alleviating
jet-tag is to open up with childlike curiosity.

One spring evening in New Delhi I was invited to
attend an opulent wedding. A huge mansion was fes-
tooned with flowers and populated with bejewelled

guests. To the blaring of trumpets, the bridegroom, wearing a breastplate of pure gold, rode in on a white horse, escorted by an entourage of male friends and relatives sporting pastel-colored silk dinner jackets.

Servants peppered the room with silver platters of delicious food. "Don't you notice?" my host pointed out. "See, they are only offering potatoes." This wedding took place during Mrs. Gandhi's first term, with its numerous austerity measures, one of which forbade hosts at large gatherings to serve anything but potatoes!

There were *pakoras* (deep fried); *kebab* (marinated and grilled); *bhaji* (with mustard seeds, coriander, and coconut); *dum* (with yogurt, ginger, cloves, and cinnamon); *song* (with tamarind); and *paratha* (mashed inside a sandwich).

I've had countless wonderful meals in India. When I think of India, my mouth starts to water. Ironically, people from India can go hungry in the West, due to jet-tag. For example, when my friend visited California, he told me, he nearly starved. At meal times his hosts asked him, "Are you hungry?" Out of politeness he had to say, "No," despite his hunger.

"In India," he explained to me, "unless a host tries to coax you to eat, it is not polite to accept."

In flight, one night, during a dinner service, a tall, Scandinavian man signaled me in a way which I interpreted to mean, *I'm done; take this away*. As I approached him, I said, by way of confirmation, "Sir, are you finished?"

"No, no," he said, "I'm Swedish."

Cultural differences are often funny, and sometimes they can be turned to advantage. For instance, in Japan people are quite fanatical about cleanliness, a sanitary consciousness which is evident even at Narita Airport, where customs agents invariably wave a person on with a white-gloved hand rather than look through a bag that has dirty laundry on top.

✈ If you don't want your bag examined in Japan, just sneeze over it as the agent approaches you!

Worldwide, customs agents tune into body language in order to separate travelers with symptoms of jetlag from smugglers with intentions which zigzag.

✈ To expedite customs clearance anywhere, display friendly body language; smile and lean towards your agent.

Over the years, as I've moved around the planet, I've kept an eye on the world's progressing homogenization as an ongrowing current of events. Cultural differences, like endangered species, are rapidly disappearing. For many years, I traveled with a camera to try to record cultural anomalies. Photography offers a beautiful metaphor for travelers. For instance, when taking a picture, we can keep what's unimportant (to us) out of focus, simply by using a close-up lens or a shallow depth of field. In the same way, when our hearts are in focus — when love fills the heart — the journey becomes both a means and an end.

AERODYNAMIC ATTITUDE (Positive Stress)

In probing the subject of jetters' stress, we meet the final dragon in this text — Aviation Super Stress (the ASS dragon). Travelers either harness this monster and ride it, or get burned by its fiery breath. Burning symptoms include back problems, headache, and glitches in the gastro-intestinal tract. Those possessed by ASS are soon consumed and, thence, become asses to all and sundry.

Harnessed ASS (HA) results in a powerful state of well-being. One remains light, while functioning effectively in the immediate reality of the moment.

We have seen how a traveler's well-being (physical,

mental, emotional, and spiritual) is impacted by jet trav-el. This also works in reverse: how we choose to adjust to the multiple stressors of jetlag, jet-snag, and jet-tag impacts our journey at every stage and on every level.

Here's a little test. Picture yourself accomplishing the following travel tasks; as you *observe* yourself, imagine you can actually *feel* your level of stress. What are you like as you research air fares? Make decisions on cli-mate, hotel, transportation, and recreation at your des-tination? Is packing and handling baggage a struggle or a juggle? Do you like to leave your house a certain way, or in disarray? Take care of mail? Your auto? Last will and testament?

At the airport, how do you greet the agent? Do you face delay with equanimity? Bristle at security? How's it on the runway, waiting for a takeoff slot with no circu-lating air? Eating and sleeping off schedule? Exploring new ways of being? Smiling or sulking?

When we jet, we need to be prepared to meet stress, for stress has never been, nor will it ever be, denied a boarding pass. Stress stows away when we jet away. Unticketed, it slips right past security. Our security — similar to the guards at airports worldwide who con-scientiously X-ray carry-ons in an effort to impede terrorists — is probably equally underpaid for such an awesome responsibility! (Aviation analysts now implore us to start manning these positions with highly-paid, multi-lingual specialists.)

✈ Prevent stress from stowing away on your journey. Pay your security its fair wage by paying attention to how you feel.

In our normal waking life, as we taxi the runways of being, moving here and there to make way for others and to advance into place towards our goals, we find, ironically, that it's often the stressors (such as lack of money, unrequited love, even illness) which empower us to soar.

Similarly, a jet must overcome what would otherwise keep it down, the stressor *drag*. In aerodynamics, lift is revealed in the resistance to drag.[151]

Additionally, aircraft engineers deliberately introduce stress into an aircraft's flexing skeleton; this creates tenacity beyond the potential strength of individual parts. Humans, too, are endowed with tenacity beyond our apparent strength. Time and again we prove fit to carry whatever weight is placed upon us.

Even literally — for example, on takeoff when we must sustain an increased g-force (gravity weight), we adapt so naturally that we hardly notice it.

On the ground we all weigh 1 g. Then, on ascent, we weigh between 1.5 and 3 g, depending on the aircraft's speed and its angle of climb. With 3.0 gs, for instance, a person weighing in at 125 pounds on Earth, will momentarily feel the massiveness of 375 pounds.

Maximum human tolerance is defined as "5 g for 5 seconds," when blood pools in legs and hearts are incapable of pumping enough back up to feed brains with oxygen. The result is loss of vision, then loss of consciousness, unless you're wearing one of those special g-suits designed for fighter pilots!

On commercial jets, as increased gs thrust us backwards against our seats, our blood also tends to pool a little in the legs, resulting in a slightly decreased flow of oxygen to the brain.

✈ Increased gs on takeoff is a lightheaded opportunity to fly through the door to dream state.

✈ Takeoff is the easiest time all flight to fall asleep, if you're ready. (See HOW TO SLEEP ON JETS, page 127.)

✈ Passengers who prefer not to dream or sleep, who

want to re-awaken their brains immediately, can squeeze their calves.

G-force, though it only lasts a minute or so and can be so negligible that we usually ignore it, can also serve as a turning point towards metaphysical thought. Try this on for size: how much we *feel* we weigh is an opportunity to change our perceptions. For example, people who have dieted off fifty pounds usually experience accompanying, transformative personality shifts. Or, going in the other direction, when a slight person suddenly weighs 375 pounds, even for a moment, s/he can use this magnification to see through form into what is generally invisible and unavailable.

➤ Take advantage of the turning point of takeoff. As the aircraft climbs, we have a few precious moments to jettison everything which no longer serves us, even old ways of thinking — our excess baggage from the past in the form of guilts and fears — along with the dark smoke the jets spew.

The letter g has so many meanings in the English language: it's an abbreviation for "good" in grading and for "general audience" in motion picture ratings. It's a musical key, a thousand dollars, and a focus spot in tantric sex — gee whiz! As with all things, there are so many ways to look at it. In the end, the choice is simply up to us.

Like an airplane, the body can fly high or fly low. It is up to us to deliberately employ jetlag as a tension-loaded springboard. It is up to us what kind of journey we have. We can choose to race through airports, bristle at delays, down cocktails (later regretted) while en route, arrive with swollen guts, toss and turn that night, nod off at meetings, misdirect anger, and blame it all on jetlag.

Or, we can choose to play a part in aviation safety and health, and feel better doing it. We can choose to say, Jetlag, that Laggin' Dragon, has been tamed!

How To Sleep On Jets

Watching the various ways people sleep on jets was always a fascination of mine when I was flying. As I plowed the aisles on nightflights, I used to wonder, In what other job could someone see thousands of people asleep?

Take celebrities, for instance. They are so much less larger-than life when asleep. I remember the actor, Dick Van Dyke, snoring away with his mouth open wide all the way to London. I remember one of the Miss Universes, refused to even recline her seat and put her head on a pillow. She said she couldn't mess her hair, as the press would be at our arrival airport. Then there was a famous forties nightclub crooner, in the sixties, under an undulating blanket, with a girlfriend.

On nightflights many passengers drape over armrests, as limp as empty garment bags. Some pass out on the floor by exits, only to be roused by the next passing flight attendant.

I remember two men, one awake, the other asleep on his friend's shoulder — well, not exactly. I was serving soft drinks from a large tray. As the first man took his, I suggested, "Would you like to take an extra for your friend when he wakes up?"

His response: "I have never met this man before." Yet, he didn't wake the stranger who found comfort on his shoulder.

For some passengers, sleeping upright in an airplane seat is an impossible dream. It used to be for me, too. Now, however, I've had so much practice — during breaks when working long-hauls and, of course, on days off, taking advantage of my pass privileges.

My technique for sleeping in an economy airplane seat involves a certain investment in preparation. If you've been unable to sleep in jets, I'm sure you'll also find this investment worthwhile — especially on red-eyes eastbound where sleep en route expedites jetlag clearance. For those passengers who have trouble sleeping on jets, there's time lost catching up later. The fine art of sleeping aloft can definitely impact the overall success of a journey.

Packing Prep. Include in carry-on: 1) bottle of drinking water, 2) eye-mask with the words *Do Not Disturb* written or taped on it, 3) ear plugs, 4) sweater or shawl, 5) socks), 6) large cotton hanky, 7) inflatable neck pillow, 8) carbohydrate snack, 9) oil, and 10) toiletries' kit (toothbrush, moisturizer, etc.).

Boarding. If you're scouting a place to stretch out, check the armrests in a row before claiming it; usually front rows of each section, for example, don't have armrests which pull out or even raise up. Also, the seatbacks in front of emergency-exit rows generally don't recline at all.

Stow your carry-on under the seat in front of you.

Find a pillow and a blanket. The airlines provide only one pillow and one blanket per aircraft seat, at the most. During boarding, check the overhead bin nearest you; if it's empty, check others — they are not assigned. You can claim one pillow and one blanket from anywhere in your class. However, economy passengers will be chastised if they try to take a cloth-covered pillow or large-sized blanket from business or first. If you don't find your set, query attendants; there's usually a stash.

Take your seat.

Prior To Takeoff. Nibble your snack. (Optional, to help with your resolve to skip meal service.)

Swaddle yourself with sweater, socks, and airline mini-blanket, to create cocoon-like privacy.

Fasten seatbelt loosely outside blanket.

Blow up inflatable pillow.

Ready ear plugs and eye-mask to don on ascent.

Practice: un-velcro headrest cushion, re-velcro it.

Oil nostrils. Moisturize hands and face.

Wet hanky from own bottle of drinking water. Cover nose and mouth with hanky for personal humidity.

Takeoff. Fully recline seat as aircraft wheels leave the runway.

Un-velcro headrest cushion. Re-position it behind the small of your back, to create a few extra inches of recline.

Place little airline pillow behind your head. Cradle your neck in inflatable pillow.

Position carry-on as footrest.

Don eye-mask and ear plugs.

Tell subconscious: Wake me at the top of descent (cued by the engines whining a higher pitch).

Doze off with the extra g-force of ascent, counting sheep or muttering a magic incantation, such as: *I easily slumber in the sanctum of the Almighty Pilot who sings me a lullaby of jet hum and humdrum.*

If you wake up early due to dryness, wet hanky again, and resume deep sleep.

Top Of Descent. Wake up. Get up. Use lav. (They are usually quite empty until the first landing announcements are made, about fifteen minutes from now.)

Clean teeth. Splash cold water on face and hands (from faucet, not sink bowl). Re-moisturize skin.

Circuit the plane for exercise. Groucho walk.

Return to seat. Fold blanket. Re-velcro headrest cushion.

Sip water.

FLYANA'S AVIATION EXAMINATION

Part I. MUTIPLE CHOICE

1) Alternate names for jetlag are:
   A. Cabotage.
   B. Circadian desynchronization.
   C. Dysrhythmia.
   D. Dimwits' Disease.

2) A New York to Tokyo nonstop flight:
   A. When we include the ground time driving to/from airports, may take twenty-four hours.
   B. Does not have a smoke-free zone because Japanese people, in general, love to smoke.
   C. Is the longest nonstop in the world.
   D. Arrives at an airport out in the *boonies*.

3) Airlines don't permit these people to sit near exits:
   A. Deaf passengers.
   B. Most Samoan passengers.
   C. Hand-cuffed prisoners accompanied by armed guards.
   D. Elizabeth Taylor.

4) The "best" seat on a jet is:
   A. Near a lavatory.
   B. By a window.
   C. On an aisle.
   D. Next to Elizabeth Taylor.

5) Airline policy regarding traveling with a pet is:
   A. Only one cat, dog, or bird is permitted in each air-craft cabin.
   B. Pets must remain in closed, sealed containers throughout flights.
   C. A seeing-eye dog is not considered a pet; it may accompany a blind passenger without additional charge.
   D. Seeing-eye dogs are too large to ride in commercial jet cabins and must fly below deck, in cargo holds.

6) Airline policy regarding children:
   A. Children five years old may travel alone on non-stops.
   B. Children under two must be held whenever the seatbelt sign is turned on.
   C. Children under eleven always get a 20% discount.
   D. Children flying alone may never sit in first class.

7) The "English muffin standard" is:
   A. A first-class breakfast service on flights to London.
   B. A flight attendants' test for food doneness.
   C. A controllers' term for ruffled low-cumulus clouds.
   D. A standard term for radiation exposure.

8) The word embarkation defines the following:
   A. Receiving a boarding pass.
   B. Everything which takes place between arriving at an airport and boarding a jet.
   C. Going to ARRIVALS to depart because you've just arrived at the airport.
   D. Being chased by a pack of dogs.

9) In flight, each first class passenger:
   A. Has his own emergency exit.
   B. Enjoys three times more air than economy travelers.
   C. Gets to visit the cockpit whenever he wants.
   D. Is rich and/or famous.

10) Changing seats in flight enables one to:
   A. Sleep lying down across several seats.
   B. Get the best seat in the "house" for the movie.
   C. Receive a meal sooner.
   D. Receive a second meal.

11) We may operate these electronic devices on jets:
   A. Handheld computer games.
   B. Cellular phones.
   C. Remote-controlled toys.
   D. Vibrators.

12) The first movie ever shown in flight was:
   A. *The High and the Mighty* starring John Wayne.
   B. Introduced by SAFE Airlines.
   C. Introduced in the sixties.
   D. Introduced in the thirties, a silent film, which was perfect because headsets hadn't been invented yet.

13) If you feel nausea and dizziness two hours after landing the cause could be:
   A. Perilymph fistula.
   B. The flu caught from another passenger.
   C. Food poisoning.
   D. Culture shock.

14) To *complete a dive* in airline jargon means:
   A. To fly to a tropical locale and learn to snorkel.
   B. In flight, to suddenly lose altitude, then level off.
   C. To be under a drip from the ceiling in the main cabin caused by a leaky upper-deck lav.
   D. To frequent bars where airline pilots hang out.

15) Stewardesses were introduced into airline service:
   A. On Playboy Airlines in the fifties.
   B. After the first incident of passenger airsickness.
   C. During World War II.
   D. In the thirties by a nurse named Church.

16) Are you a "power flyer?"
   A. You are a member of three bonus-award programs.
   B. You don't hesitate to write the airlines if you think an employee has stepped out of line.
   C. You make all your smart-class preparations in a timely manner to avoid anxiety.
   D. Sometimes, angels with two sets of wings visit you.

17) U.S. Customs Service:
   A. Pays informers 25% of the amount recovered from any cheating traveler.
   B. Occasionally disrobes people to examine body cavities.
   C. Performs their work enthusiastically in pursuit of truth, justice, and the American way.
   D. Has keys for every type of luggage in the world.

18) Which amenities are available on the U.S. president's Air Force One and not on commercial airlines?
   A. Shower.
   B. Paper shredder.
   C. Kingsize bed.
   D. Shrimp peeler.

19) The Mile High Club is made up of people who:
   A. At one time or other, have made love on a jet.
   B. Have taken off from Denver Stapleton Airport.
   C. Leave magazines under sinks in commercial jet lavs, so other members will have something to read in there.
   D. Meditate daily.

20) "If I had to choose, I would rather have birds than airplanes," was said by:
   A. Charles Lindberg.
   B. Amelia Earhart.
   C. Henry Audubon.
   D. Juan Trippe.

Part II. ANSWERS TO MULTIPLE CHOICE

1) B and C are true; scientific names to define the lack of synchronicity between the environmental (outer) clock and a jetter's (inner) biological clock. Cabotage is when a foreign airline operates domestic flights in another country. Jetlag is caused by changes in light and does affect the brain, possibly resulting in the creation of such spurious answers as Dimwits' Disease.

2) A is true. New York/Tokyo takes 13:50 hours; longer nonstops are San Francisco/Hong Kong (14:00) and Los Angeles/Sydney (14:35). Other double digit long-hauls include Riyadh/New York (12:35) and Johannesburg/ Lisbon (11:35). Although Narita Airport is a few hours by train from Tokyo, it is definitely not the *boonies*. Rather, it sits in a lovely rural area with charming shops, a temple, and a traffic signal at the main inter-section of town which plays music as it changes — a humane innovation for the blind, and jetlagged!

3) A, B and C are true. The airlines hand-pick those whom they seat by exits; these people are projected to be, in an emergency, agile enough to open an exit, and open enough to take directions from a female (70% of attendants are women). According to airline thinking this excludes the deaf, blind, handicapped, pregnant, infirm, and obese. Samoans are not obese, but big (nine out of ten requires a seatbelt extension). Parents and

armed guards are eliminated, too, because they're pre-occupied. D is false; everyone knows Elizabeth Taylor can sit anywhere she wants.

4) All answers are correct; it's a personal choice.

5) B, C, and D are true. C applies to domestic U.S. flights; D is international. A is false because two kittens or puppies are allowed per cabin if they are under ten-weeks old, and two birds are always permitted in the same cabin if they are in the same container. Most 747s have six cabins divided by bulkhead panels: first, business, three economy, and one upper deck (designated any class).

6) Only A is correct. Children under two may be held during takeoff/turbulence, or may also sit in a car seat strapped into a passenger seat. Children only sometimes get a 20% discount, depending on routing and never unaccompanied. Children may ride first class, with a discount.

7) Only D is true.

8) Only B is true. A is incomplete. C is confused think-ing (premature jetlag). D is more or less a homonym.

9) Only B is counted true for the purpose of this quiz. A could be, if there were only two passengers in first class; which is often populated with frequent flyers, famous or not, cashing in mileage awards.

10) A, B and C are true, excellent reasons to change seats. D isn't; meals are synced with passenger loads — which doesn't leave a lot of room for the extra-hungry, or for burning/spillage/pillage.

11) A and D are true. Other "acceptables": calculators, heart pacemakers, hearing aids, shavers, and cassette tape players. Radios are not; a passenger who refused to

turn off his portable radio when asked (10/91) was convicted of a federal offense, punishable up to ten months
in prison.[152] B and C are also no-no. The airlines claim
remote devices (including cellular phones) interfere
with navigation. However, the FCC recently reported
that this so-called navigational interference is merely
"anecdotal."[153]

12) C is true. Airlines edit all films, cutting profanity,
nudity, politics, religion, and, of course, airline crashes. There really was a SAFE Airlines (Southwest Air
Fast Express) in 1929; it has since bit the dust. You
may not have heard of a lot of commercial air carriers.
As of 2/92, there were 724 airlines operating around
the world.[154]

13) A, B and C are true. Perilymph fistula is an inner ear
leak which can happen from rapid change in air pressure
on descent. Doctors report many passengers catch the flu
when traveling. (See STOP BUGGING ME, page 70.) I've
seen only three cases of food poisoning. D is false; culture
shock can be dizzying, but never nauseating.

14) Only B is true. A: on a reef. B: with great relief.
C: gees! D: mischief.

15) D is true; Ellen Church originated the idea and she
was among the original eight, all nurses. At that time,
other suggested names for stewardess were airette, airess,
airmaid, airaide, aidette, courierette, and hostess. The
label "flight attendant" began to stick in the seventies,
when the profession became unisex. *Playboy* has probably done more damage to the image of stewardesses
than any single flight attendant on a bad day.

16) A, C and D are counted true for the purpose of this
quiz. B, on the other hand, is a grumbling flyer, taking
advantage of the fact that the airlines dispense disci-

plinary action rather liberally, adhering to the time-honored belief that "the customer is always right."

17) All answers are true; knowing this is smart.

18) A and B are counted true. The presidential jet does not have a kingsize bed, rather two twin beds.[155] However, MGM Grand Air, which flies between New York and California, boasts a queensize bed. D is presently classified.

19) A and D are counted true. There are, in fact, loose organizations (without newsletters) of travelers who've probed the depths of these questions and feel that these are the correct answers.

20) A is true. Who is Juan Trippe? Is he the guy whose name coined the term "roundtrip"? Juan Trippe was the visionary who birthed Pan Am in 1927, and then proceeded to open commercial air lanes to every corner of the globe.

Part III. A HIGHER ALTITUDE

There are forty correct answers to this quiz. If you'd like to go further, take the second word from correct answers, sequentially, 3, 29, and 38. Now see the sentence they form. You can check yourself by finding this sentence in the second paragraph on page 82.

Dragon Wisdom

I count my Blessings and do my best. I have faith that the Almighty Pilot takes care of the rest.

Only feelings of peace and security enter me through the air waves and the All Ways.

I experience the creativity and affluence of the Divine Design as It manifests around me and through me.

I relax in rarefied atmosphere high above the clouds. Only Exquisite Energy distills to me from this air. I thrive on the quality of air I breathe.

I tune in to changes in sound and pressure as aspects of the Grand Composer. I ensure that the hums and haws which I caw are nourishing for others.

I am much more than my body; my essence travels faster to any place in the world than any plane in the sky.

STAMPS

The postage stamps used as illustrations in this text are from my own collection. When I was flying I used to wander into philatelic shops all over the world. Just about every stamp which caught my eye had an airplane on it.

There was one dealer in Osaka who had a lot of airmail stamps. It was easy for me to swing by there on my layovers because he was located near our hotel. I'd spend about 2000 yen (around $6 in those days) on a couple of treasures. On my third visit, the dealer initiated conversation for the first time. "You live Osaka?"

"No, I'm with Pan Am."

"Ah, So. Pan Am. Very few Pan Am stamps."

I thought of my stamp from Pago Pago with the pontooned clipper sitting in a lagoon, and one lone native in a canoe paddling towards it. I remembered how thrilled I was when I first saw it, and also the one I found from Hungary, issued in 1977, featuring our 747 with the blue ball on its tail. "Oh, you have Pan Am stamps?" I asked excitedly.

He nodded and crossed the room, opened a large box, pulled out an album, wrong one, pulled out another, right one. He half-ran towards me, and proudly placed the open page on the counter. There they were, rows and rows of stamps from Panama.

Stamps in order of appearance:

France, 1946-47, Iris, Messenger Goddess, title page.

Australia, 1991, Golden Days of Radio, p3.

Hong Kong, 1985, Dragon Boat Festival, p21.

Hungary, 1942, Planes and Ghostly Chiefs, p51.

Nicaragua, 1978, Icarus Flew Too Close to the Sun, p53.

Benin, 1977, Concorde Supersonic Plane, p66.

Montserrat, 1971, Plane and Stewardesses, p73.

New Zealand, 1963-64, Plane Spraying Farmland, p90.

People's Republic of China, 1980, Jet on a Runway, p101.

Germany, 1943, Nazi Dive Bombers, p106.

Egypt, 1933-38, Airplane over Giza Pyramids, p119.

Uruguay, 1930, Pegasus, The Flying Horse, p127.

Iraq, 1966, Couple on a Magic Carpet Ride, p131.

Switzerland, 1935-38, Allegorical Figure of Flight, p139.

Liberia, 1974, Mail Runner and Jet, p140.

Tunisia, 1983, Woman with Jet Sunglasses, p155.

Thanks to Rick Medcalf, Island Coin and Stamp, Lahaina, Maui, for researching the dates of these stamps.

BIBLIOGRAPHY

DRAGON BREATH (What Is Jetlag?)

1. Martindale, David, "Must Passengers Make Do with Mediocrity?" *Frequent Flyer*, 1/88, p50.

2. Winget, C.M., Ph.D., "Desynchronosis," Navy Aerospace Physiologist Meeting, Flight Stress/Fatigue/Performance Period, 10/16-18/73.

3. Wellborn, Stanley N., "For Too Many, Life Is Just a Snore," *U.S. News & World Report*, 6/15/87, p56.

4. Zverina, Ivan, "John Foster Dulles and Jet Lag," UPI News, New York, 3/15/88.

5. *Maui News*, "Fight Over Airline Armrest Leads to Assault Arrest," 10/24/90.

DRAGON'S DEN (Nature and Body Clocks)

6. Strughold, M.D., Hubertus, *Your Body Clock, Its Significance for the Jet Traveler*, Charles Scribner's Sons, 1971, p19.

LAGGIN' DRAGON (Disruption of Body Clocks)

7. Luce, Gay Gaer, *Body Time, Physiological Rhythms and Social Stress*, Random House, 1971, pp136-7.

8. Strughold, *Your Body Clock*, p45.

9. Greist, M.D., John H. and Georgia L., *Fearless Flying*, Nelson-Hall, 1981, p69.

10. McFarland, Ross, "Air Travel across Time Zones," *Aerospace Medicine*, 6/74, 45:648.

11. Cogan, M.D., John, Honolulu cardiologist, telephone conversations and correspondence with permission.

THE NATURE OF THE BEAST (Flying East or West)

12. Coleman, Richard M., *Wide Awake at 3:00 A.M.*, W.H. Freeman & Co., 1986, p69.

DRAGON LOADSTONE (Magnetic Fields)

13. Sherson, Robbie, author and retired First Mate, New

Zealand Merchant Marines, conversations with permission.

14. Evans, John, *Mind, Body and Electromagnetism*, Element Books Ltd., 1986, p147.

THE DRAGON'S TALE (Travel Experience)

15. Ehret, Dr. Charles and Lynne Waller Scanlon, *Overcoming Jet Lag*, Berkley Publishing, New York, 1983, p149.

16. McFarland, "Air Travel across Time Zones," 45:648.

17. Carruthers, M.D., Malcolm, A.E. Arguelles, M.D., Abraham Mosovich, M.D., "Man In Transit: Biochemical and Physiological Changes During Intercontinental Flight," *The Lancet*, 5/8/76, p980.

18. Miller, Susan, "Cosmic Radiation and Other Crew Health Issues," Association of Flight Attendants, National Health Committee Report, 1/90.

19. Majendie, Paul, "Heinz 'Bean Baron' Tony O'Reilly, Frenetic Globetrotter," Reuter, Dublin, 10/31/91.

20. Suplee, Curt, "Eliminating Witnesses; Lawmakers May Aim Questions at TV Screens in the Future," Washington Post, 11/7/91.

PIE IN THE SKY (Travel Diet)

21. Ehret, *Overcoming Jet Lag*, p149.

22. Houston, M.D., Charles S., "Going High, The Story of Man and Altitude," The American Alpine Club, New York, p104.

23. Siegel, Dr. Peter V. (Air Surgeon, FAA), Dr. Siegfried J. Gerathewohl (Chief of Research Planning, FAA), Dr. Stanley R. Mohler (Chief of Aeromedical Applications, FAA), "Time-Zone Effects," address at American Association for the Advancement of Science, 12/30/67.

24. *Traveling Healthy & Comfortably*, 108-48 70th Road, Forest Hills, New York 11375, Vol.4, # 1, 1/91, p1.

25. Greenberg, Peter S., "Airline Food," *Frequent Flyer*, 1/92, p26.

BIKINIS & FURS (Meteorological Virtues)

26. Winfree, Arthur, "Lighting Up the body Clock," Shawna

Vogel, *Discover*, 1/90.

27. Czeisler, Dr. Charles and Professor Richard Kronauer, "Jet Lag Breakthrough," *Conde Nast Traveler*, 9/89, p35.

28. Irwin, M.D., Michael, Medical Director United Nations, "Jet lag afflicts many but few know the cure," *Star Bulletin*, 3/20/88.

29. Robbins, John, *Diet For a New America*, Stillpoint, 1987, p58.

CELESTIAL SLUMBER (Sleep At Night)

30. Blask, Ann Sabatini, "The Pro on the Go," *Frequent Flyer*, 5/90, p98.

31. Rensberger, Boyce, "Effects of Halcion on Bush Discounted; Drug Used for Jet Lag Subject of Controversy," *Washington Post*, 1/9/92.

32. Reuter News, Washington, "Bush Has Stopped Taking Controversial Sleeping Pills," 2/5/92.

33. Reuter News, Moscow, "Three Days, Four Cities — Yeltsin's Crucial Test," 1/29/92.

34. Forbes, Mary Ann, "Baptism By Fire: Michelle Honda's Grueling Test Reveals Flight Attendants as Safety Professionals," *Flightlog*, Association of Flight Attendants, AFL-CIO, Vol.26, No. 2, 1988, p3.

35. "Harvard Medical School Health Letter," 3/88, 13(5), p8.

36. *Union Update*, Association of Flight Attendants, 11/90, p18.

37. *Lancet*, "Jet lag and its Pharmacology," 8/30/86, p494.

38. Arendt, Mary, "Facing Up to Travel," *Frequent Flyer*, 3/91, p26.

39. Winget, Ph.D., C.M. and Joan Vernikos Danellis, "Desynchronosis," Environmental Biology Division, Ames Research Center, NASA, 4/16/76.

40. Bryant, Samuel, "What Jet Travel Does to your Metabolic Clock," *Fortune*, 11/63.

LET YOUR SPIRIT SOAR! (Meditation)

41. *The New York Times*, 11/15/88.

THE AIRBORNE HABITAT (Compounding Jetlag)

42. *Daily Planet Almanac*, 1981, "Jet Lag," p41.

43. Werjefelt, Bertil, presentation to Senate Aviation Subcommittee, "The Air That Passengers Breathe," *Frequent Flyer*, 11/85, p100.

DROWNING IN MID AIR (Altitude)

44. Poppy, John, "Air Travail," *Esquire*, 9/89, p142.

45. Kahn, F.S., *The Curse of Icarus*, Routledge, 1990, p62.

46. Hiernaux, Jean, "Man at High Altitude," *Man in the Heat, High Altitude, and Society*, Charles C. Thomas, 1982, p27.

47. Karpilow, Dr. Craig, "How the Diabetic Can Best Cope with Jet Lag," *The Diabetic Traveler*, P.O. Box 8223 RW, Stamford, CT 06905, Autumn 1981, p6.

48. Gullet, M.D., Charles, *Journal of the American Medical Association* reprinted in *Vogue*, 2/81, p197.

TO PEE OR NOT TO PEE (Dehydration)

49. Davidson, M.A., John, Wholistic Research Company, Catalog of Environmental & Natural Health Care Products & Books, Bright Haven, Robin's Lane, Lolworth, Cambridge CB3 BHH, England.

50. Best, A.S., Pan American World Airways Air Conditioning Tests During Revenue Flights, Boeing Report No. T6-4453-B747SP, 1976, reprinted in *Aviation, Space, and Environmental Medicine*, 2/80, p170.

51. Rippe, M.D., James, PR Newswire, 2/24/89.

52. Irwin, "Jet Lag Afflicts Many But Few Know The Cure."

53. Adams, Anne L., "Every Hair in Place," *Frequent Flyer*, 10/91, p30.

54. Xenex Corporation: Aircraft Humidification, "Aircraft-Specific Climate Factors," *Kitty Hawk*, Aviation Safety & Health Association, 1001 Bishop Street, Suite 910, Honolulu, HI 96813, No.13, 1/89, p2.

55. Rowan, Roy, "Jet Lag Isn't Just A State Of Mind," *Fortune*, 4/76.

56. *Maui News*, AP Minneapolis, "Airline Crew Imbibed Heavily before Flight," 8/1/90.

57. Nelson, Margaret, "Alcohol-Airline Case goes to Trial," *USA Today*, 7/23/90, 3A.

58. *Aviation Week & Space Technology*, "Female Aerospace Employment," 6/10/91, p11.

ZAP! (Radiation)

59. Orloski, Ph.D., Ray F., Founding Trustee of the Pritikin Institute, "Some Thoughts on Jet Lag," ARI Newsletter, with permission to print from Jim Fahey, Biotec Food Corporation, 3638 Waialae Ave., Honolulu, Hi 96816, no date.

60. Gridley, Peter, "Radiation Alert: Will Flying Give You Cancer?" *Glamour*, 5/90, p196.

61. *Airliner Cabin Environment, Air Quality and Safety*, Committee on Airliner Cabin Air Quality, Board on Environmental Studies and Toxicology, Commission on Life Sciences, National Research Counsel, National Academy Press, Washington, D.C., 1986, p119.

62. Barish Ph.D., Robert J., *Understanding In-Flight Radiation*, In-Flight Radiation Protection Services, Inc., 211 East 70th Street, New York, NY 10021, 4/89, p55.

63. Donsbach, Kurt W., Ph.D., D.Sc., N.D., D.C. and Richard O. Brennan, D.O., "Superoxide Dismutase," International Institute of Natural Health Sciences, Inc., 7422 Mountjoy Drive, Huntington Beach, CA 92648, 1982, p14.

64. *Flightlog*, "Flight Attendant Health Issues for 1990," Association of Flight Attendants, AFL-CIO, 1-3/90, p11.

65. Luxembourg, "The Cosmic Radiation Environment at Air Carrier Flight Altitudes and Possible Associate Health Risks," Workshop on Radiation Exposure of Civil Aircrew, 6/25-27/91.

66. Barish, *Understanding In-Flight Radiation*, p39.

67. FAA, U.S. Department of Transportation, "Radiation Exposure of Air Carrier Crewmembers," AAM-624, 3/5/90.

OH! ZONED (Ozone)

68. Subcommittee on Oversight and Investigations, U.S. House of Representatives, "Adverse Health Effects of Inflight Exposure to Atmospheric Ozone," 7/18/79, p11.

69. Cohen, Carol and Pat Morrissey, "Persistence Results in Ozone Rule," *Passenger & Inflight Service*, Box 188, Hialeah, Fl 33011, 12/80, p13.

70. Kahn, *The Curse of Icarus*, p106.

71. Subcommittee on Oversight and Investigations, p23.

72. Cone, M.D., M.P.H., James E., "Cabin Air Casualties: A Flight Attendant Health Survey," *Kitty Hawk*, No.4, 2/86, p2.

73. *Airliner Cabin Environment*, p119.

STOP BUGGING ME (Airborne Contaminants)

74. Poppy, John, "Air Travail," *Esquire*, 9/89, p142.

75. Garrard, Alice, "What Ails You?" quoting Dr. David Silverman of New York University School of Medicine, *Frequent Flyer*, 3/88, pp42-44.

76. Mar, M.D., Jacque, JAMA, 11/20/87, Vol 258, No.19, p2764.

77. *Airliner Cabin Environment*, p196.

78. Winget, Ph.D., C.M. and Joan Vernikos Danellis, "Desynchronosis," Environmental Biology Division, Ames Research Center, NASA, 4/16/76, p8.

79. *Airliner Cabin Environment*, p156.

80. *Airliner Cabin Environment*, p7.

BOTTOM LINE VS LIFELINE (Fuel-Saving)

81. Trask, Peter, "Aviation Safety And Health," *Kitty Hawk*, No.2, 11/85, p1.

82. *Airliner Cabin Environment*, p43.

83. McFarland, Ross and J.N. Evans, "Alterations in Dark Adaptation under Reduced Oxygen Tensions," *American Journal of Physiology*, 1939, 127(1):37-50.

84. McFarland, Ross, "Experimental Evidence of the Relationship Between Aging and Oxygen Want: In Search of

a Theory of Aging," *Ergonomics*, 1963, 6(4):339-66.

85. *Union Update*, Association of Flight Attendants, 12/88, p5.

86. *Consumer Reports*, 1990 Annual Questionnaire, "The Best (and Worst) Airlines," 7/91, p462.

87. Alter, Joseph D. and Stanley R. Mohler, "Preventive Medicine Aspects and Health Promotion Programs for Flight Attendants, *Aviation, Space, and Environmental Medicine*, 2/80, p172.

88. Irwin, M.D., Michael, Medical Director World Bank, *Washington Monthly*, 6/90, p34.

89. *Airliner Cabin Environment*, p43.

90. Gong Jr., MD, Henry, "Advising Patients With Pulmonary Diseases on Air Travel," *Annals of Internal Medicine*, Vol 111, Number 5, p350.

91. Beauchamp, Marc, "Asleep on the Job", *Forbes*, 5/30/88, p292.

92. Leon, Cheryle, president of Association of Professional Flight Attendants, *Aviation Week & Space Technology*, 3/18/91, p23.

93. Hochschild, Professor Arlie Russell, *The Managed Heart*, University of California Press, 1983, pp93-4.

94. *Eastwest Journal*, 9/89, p10.

AGE BEFORE DUTY (Aging Fleet)

95. Martindale, David, *Frequent Flyer*, "How Safe is the Fleet?" 5/89, p36.

96. *Aviation Week & Space Technology*, 12/10/90, p15.

97. TIME, 11/7/88, "Cracking Down, The FAA Orders Overhauls to Make Aging 737s Safer," p105.

98. *Aviation Week & Space Technology*, 4/8/91, p13.

HUB RUB (Transits)

99. *Consumer Reports*, 1990 Annual Questionnaire, p465.

100. *Frequent Flyer*, "What Business Travelers Really Think," 12/91, p39.

101. *Fly-Rights*, Civil Aeronautics Board, 1982, p7.

102. Zagat U.S. Travel Survey, 1991, Eugene H. Zagat, Jr. and Nina S. Zagat, "The (Airline) World According to Zagat," *Frequent Flyer*, 1/91, p31.

KILLER MIST (Pesticide)

103. Flint, T.N., Regional Agriculture Quarantine Officer, New Zealand Ministry of Agriculture and Fisheries, personal letter to author, dated 3/29/85.

LOVE CANAL VS JET STREAM (Toxic Chemicals)

104. NELC, National Environmental Law Center, "Not All Pollution Cited," *Maui News*, 4/18/91, A9.

105. Rea, M.D., William J., David Rousseau and Jean Enwright, *Your Home, Your Health and Well-Being*, Hartley & Marks, p37.

106. *Airliner Cabin Environment*, p130.

107. Cone, "Cabin Air Casualties," p3.

108. Martindale, David, "Cargo Ignites a Controversy," *Frequent Flyer*, 11/88, pp30-2.

109. Galipault, John B., "Airliners and Hazardous Cargo ...Do You Know What's Below?" *The Aviation Safety Monitor*, Aviation Safety Institute, P.O.Box 304, Worthington, Ohio, 43085. (a non-profit organization interested in all air-safety issues: 614/885-4242), 6/90, p7.

110. *Frequent Flyer*, "Smoke Gets in Your Eyes," 2/92, p68.

111. Essex Industries, Inc., 7700 Gravois Ave., Saint Louis, Missouri, 63123-4728, 314/832-4500.

ENGLISH MUFFIN (EM Pollution)

112. Lee, Ph.D., Lita, *Radiation Protection Manual*, 3rd Ed., 1990, p33.

113. Brodeur, Paul, *The New Yorker*, "Annals of Radiation," 6/12/89, p58.

114. Smith, Cyril and Simon Best quoting William J. Rea, M.D., *Electromagnetic Man, Health & Hazard in the Electrical Environment*, St. Martin's Press, 1989, p27.

115. Cook, Wayne and Wanda, *Universal Truths*, 1988, p67.

116. Barish, *Understanding In-flight Radiation*, p84.

117. *Business Week*, 10/30/89, Safe Computing Company brochure, 368 Hillside Ave., Needham, MA 02194.

118. Brodeur, Paul, *Currents of Death*, Simon and Schuster, 1989, p130.

119. Brodeur, "Annals of Radiation," p85.

120. Lee, *Radiation Protection Manual*, pp87-88.

PUFF THE TRAGIC DRAG (Cigarettes)

121. AP, *Maui News*, "Prankster's Joke Leads to his own Federal Arrest," 2/13/91.

122. Mydans, Seth, *The New York Times* reprinted in the *Maui News*, "This is Your Captain Speaking, You Got a Light?" 3/11/90, A5.

123. Cullen, Joseph W., National Cancer Institute, "Airplane Study Finds No-Smoking Area No Help," *Honolulu Advertiser*, 2/9/89, A1.

124. Rowan, "Jetlag Isn't Just a State of Mind."

125. Clark, Kenneth, "Smokers Rights — Or Wrongs," *Frequent Flyer*, 7/89, p77.

126. *Aviation Week & Space Technology*, "Smokers Strike Back," 12/3/90, p15.

SAY WHAT? (Noise)

127. Goeltz, Judith, *Jet Stress*, International Institute of Natural Health Sciences, Huntington Beach, California, 92647, 1980, pp31-33.

128. Bronzaft, Arline, "New York Becoming a Pain in the Ear," *San Francisco Chronicle*, 8/1/90.

129. *Aviation Week & Space Technology*, "Noise Complaints," 4/22/91.

130. *The Aviation Safety Monitor*, "The Quiet New Century," 4/91, p1.

131. Glab, Jim, "Europe's Airport of the Future, Environmental opposition delayed Munich II for three decades," *Frequent Flyer*, 2/92, p21.

132. Meecham, W.C. and H.G. Smith, "Effects of Jet Aircraft Noise on Mental Hospital Admissions," *British Journal of Audiology*, 1977, 11,81-85.

133. *Aviation Week & Space Technology*, "Proposed Stage 2 Aircraft Ban Leaves Carriers and Airports in Dark over U.S. Noise Policy," 3/11/91.

18 SECONDS (Emergency)

134. *Maui News*, "The Offbeat: Bad Joke Proves Very Expensive," AP Tokyo, 4/1/91.

135. *USA TODAY*, "Fake Bomb," 7/2/90, p4A.

136. Martindale, David, "Rewriting the Book," *Frequent Flyer*, 4/89, p48.

137. Marshall, Nora C., National Transportation Safety Board, "Passenger Safety Education, Presented to the 3rd Annual International Aircraft Cabin Safety Symposium," *Kitty Hawk*, No.6, 4/86, p3.

138. Borg, Jim, "Nightmare over the Pacific," *Honolulu Star-Bulletin & Advertiser*, 2/26/89, pA-7.

139. Heftel, Cec, (Member of Congress), letter, *Kitty Hawk*, No.8, 8/86, p3.

COLD FEET (Fear of Flying)

140. FAA, *Administrator's Fact Book*, "50 Busiest Air Traffic Control Towers," 8/91, p10.

141. *Aviation Week & Space Technology*, "Assessing Human Factors," 12/3/90.

142. *Frequent Flyer*, 5/89, p33.

143. *San Francisco Chronicle*, 8/7/90.

144. *Aviation Week & Space Technology*, "Broken Bones and Frostbite," 6/18/90.

145. *Aviation Week & Space Technology*, "NTSB Blames DC-9 Crew Error for Detroit Runway Collision," 7/1/91.

146. *The Aviation Safety Monitor*, "Flight Fright," 3/92, p3.

147. Magnuson, Ed, "Brace! Brace! Brace!, *TIME*, 7/31/89, pp12-15.

148. Ibid.

149. Bunting, Jane Briggs, David Diamond, Jack Hayes, Stact D. Kramer, Steve Marsh, Stephanie Slewka, "Finding God on Flight 232," *LIFE*, 9/89, pp29-32.

150. McFarland, Ross, "Air Travel across Time Zones," 45:648.

AERODYNAMIC ATTITUDE (Positive Stress)

151. Sutton, Sir Graham, *Mastery of the Air*, Basic Books, 1965, pp13-25.

FLYANA'S AVIATION EXAMINATION

152. *The Aviation Safety Monitor*, "Checklist," 10/91, p4.

153. *Frequent Flyer*, "Travel & Technology," 10/91, p74.

154. *Aviation Week & Space Technology*, 2/3/92, p13.

155. *San Francisco Chronicle*, 9/7/90.

The Dragon Flies

THE SMART JOURNEY

Think of this section as your secretary — or maybe your grandmother. It will organize you and take care of you. It summarizes the foregoing information in step-by-step fashion, and it adds a few new pointers to keep you jet smart. Smart-class tips are now offered chronologically according to the seven stages of travel.

1) Jet Prep: plan, ticket, pack.
2) Jet Ready: car/taxi/bus/rail to airport.
3) Jet Set: check-in, security, gate, wait.
4) Jet Go: enplane, taxi, flight, taxi, deplane.
5) Jet Down: immigration, customs, baggage claim.
6) Jet Let-Go: car/taxi/bus/rail away from airport.
7) Jetlag: coping with that taxing time warp.

Of course, you don't need to do everything on this list. Every little bit helps.

If you want further information on any of these pointers, look for the words in bold. These key words can be found in the Index, which will then guide you to the appropriate section of the text.

JET PREP
(Plan, Ticket, Pack)

1) PLAN:

A) Consider these factors before choosing an airline:
- price.
- **nonstop** vs. multistop.
- flight latitude.
- departure/arrival time.
- **frequent-flyer** award.
- movie.
- aircraft type.
- terminal location.

B) Consult a good **travel agent**:
- rules/prices can literally change by the minute!
- deals are available, if you are flexible.

C) Specific handling? Supplemental **oxygen**?
   Special meal? Wheelchair?
   1 - Request your airline's **reservations**.
   2 - Ask for the **record locater number**.

D) Reserve a hotel with these amenities:
- blackout curtains.
- 24-hour room service.
- extra-large bathtubs.
- windows that open.

E) Check with your **doctor**.
- health issues (cardiovascular, **pregnancy**, etc.).
- prescribed medication dosage/timing.

2) PACK:

A) Clothes! Remember:
- do a packing **visualization**.
- research and conform to local customs.
- buy on arrival to accelerate social **cycle**.
- UNDER-PACK.
   (It's less tiring and less expensive.)

B) Prevent liquid leaks:
- *sqwoosh* air out of shampoo and other bottles.
- cover caps with masking tape.

C) For warm drink/meal in hotel room, bring:
  - heating coil.   - small rice cooker.
  - transformer.   - adapters.

D) Prep your **luggage**:
  - name & phone # outside/inside each piece.
  - hard luggage less pesticide vulnerable.
  - remove old tags.

E) Carry-on ABCs:
  - atomizer for **water**.
  - book/paperwork (already started).
  - cream for **eyes**.
  - **diode**.
  - eye-mask.
  - fan (hand or battery operated).
  - garments (inflight: sweater; arrival: locale).
  - **hanky**.
  - inflatable neck pillow.
  - JET SMART!
  - kit of toiletries.
  - layover essentials (in case of lost bag).
  - money (small bills for flight, arrival currency).
  - notes (meal preference, foreign local language).
  - **oil** for nose.
  - passport.
  - quieting **ear** plugs.
  - **remedies (flower** essences, SOD).
  - **shoe** inserts.
  - tea bags (herbal).
  - ultra-light cold formula (**niacin**, deep-heat rub).
  - **vitamins**.
  - **water** for drinking and misting.
  - **X-ray** proof (film, disk, medication) packs.
  - yummy **carbohydrate** nibbles.
  - zippered **jewelry** case.

F) Train for your **airport** trek:
- *schlep*/lift luggage for weight/size around the house.

3) BODY PREP:

A) Food: EITHER
- plan to **fast,**
  OR
- tote nutritious snacks.

B) **SOD** (for radiation):
- start one week before departure.
- 3 tablets a day.
- always on an empty stomach with a lot of **water.**

C) Night before departure:
- unload body with herbal laxative/**enema**.
- no late packing or partying!

4) **SUBTLE ENERGY**:

A) **Visualize** yourself en route/at arrival:
- happy, healthy, wise, and kind.

B) Make your commitment to the entire journey:
- to careful observation of bodily/**emotional signals**.
- to conscious management of personal effects.

C) Accelerate your social **cycle**: EITHER
- travel with significant others,
  OR
- feel that all others are significant.

5) CLEAN UP YOUR LIFE:

- Your business.
- Your home.
- Your correspondence.
- Your relationships.
  (Not necessarily in that order!)

JET READY
(Car/Taxi/Bus/Rail to **Airport**)

1) BODY PREP:

   A) Wake up:
- notify your **cycle**s that change is imminent.

   B) No caffeine:
- let the novelty of travel stimulate, instead.
- feel confident that the cosmology at your arrival destination will sufficiently stimulate your cycles.

   C) **Bathe**:
- hydrate your skin.
- relax.

   D) Dress:
- suit the departure **climate**.
- accessorize at the **airport** (out of respect).
- adjust for flight comfort (body swells, dryness).
- re-accessorize at arrival airport (**customs** easier).
- suit the arrival locale's climate/propriety.

   E) Call:
- **proton hotline** (cancel if proton event occurring).
- airline **reservations**, to check:
  - gate number,
  - possible **delay/cancellation**.

   F) Allow abundant time for possible delay.

2) **SUBTLE ENERGY**:

   A) Wear **diode,** to protect from:
- ionizing **radiation** from the **Sun**.
- non-ionizing radiation from **airport**/aircraft.

   B) Drink **flower** remedies for emotional jetlag.

   C) Wear basil sprig/fresh flower for grounding.

JET SET
(Check-in, **Security**, Gate, Wait)

1) CHECK-IN:

A) Arrive early:
- to avoid lines.
- to maximize seat preference.
- to study signage.
- to dawdle where curious.
- to negotiate maze.

B) Have these ready to offer:
- your ticket.
- your **record locater number**.
- your smile.

C) Use folding **luggage** cart:
- to move bags from curbside to check-in.
- to move carry-ons to the jet.

D) Ticket reminders:
- watch that agent uses proper 3-letter **airport code**, i.e. NRT = Narita.
- stow ticket, with claim tags, in zippered case with your money.
- only your **boarding pass** needs to be kept handy for **security**/seating.

E) Things to say to ticket agent:
- **Nonsmokers**:
    "As far away from smoke as possible."
- If you intend to **sleep**:
    "Away from **lav** and **galley**."
- If **special meal** ordered:
    "Is my special meal in the computer?"

2) **SECURITY**'S **X-RAY** STATION:

    A) Keep these from X-radiation:
- food.
- computer disks.
- photographic **film**.
- medications.

    B) Ask for manual inspection.
           (With a smile.)

    C) Keep your eyes on your personal effects.

3) WAIT AT GATE:

    A) **Exercise** to prep for hours of sitting.

    B) Rolling **delay**:
- If due to mechanical problem,
    try to change airlines.
- If due to weather/traffic,
    go for **walk**, **shower**, food, etc.

4) **SUBTLE ENERGY**:

    Begin tuning into **light**; sit by a window.

JET GO
(Enplane, Taxi, Flight, Taxi, Deplane)

1) ENPLANE:

A) Board: EITHER
- as late as possible, due to low **oxygen**,
  OR,
- early enough to greet **pilot**s on flight deck.

B) Stow **carry-on**s:
- for leg room,
  in closet or overhead compartment.
- for **footrest**,
  under seat in front.

C) **Tour** the aircraft to locate:
- **pillow/blanket**.
- **hot-water spigot**.
- magazines/newspapers.
- no-**smoking** zones.
- **lav**s.
- **fire extinguisher**s.
- exits.
- possible alternate seat.

D) Give **special meal** reminder note to attendant.
- your name.
- your meal.
- your seat number.
- your thanks!

E) Prior to taking your seat:
- remove belt.
- remove bulky objects from pockets.
- remove constricting underwear.

2) TAXI:

- A) Prepare for emergencies:
  - watch the **demo**.
  - review the folder.
  - count rows to primary/secondary exits.

- B) Fasten **seatbelt**:
  - slack, for **back** and circulation.
  - outside the **blanket**, if you **sleep**.

- C) Taxi yourself to sleep:
  - recline seat as soon as aircraft lifts off runway.
  - doze off with extra **g-force** of ascent.

3) **SLEEP**:

- A) Sleep en route according to aircraft arrival time:
  - a.m. landing, sleep aloft.
  - p.m. landing, awake aloft.

- B) Cocoon yourself:
  - cover with sweater plus airline mini-**blanket**.
  - don **eye-mask** and **ear plugs**.

- C) Extra-recline in economy:
  1 - un-velcro foam headrest.
  2 - place it behind low back.
  3 - use airline pillow for head.
  4 - use your own inflatable pillow for neck.

4) EATING ON BOARD — TWO OPTIONS:

Diet #1: One-Day **Fast**
  - no solid food.
  - gallon **water**/day.
  - **SOD** (one tablet for each hour of travel).
  - no vitamins.

Diet #2: Transition Eating
- light **carbo** snacks only when hungry.
- multi **vitamin**/mineral plus C with meals.
- liquids and SOD between meals.

- DON'T eat by old/new **clock**s.
    (Be guided by what you feel.)
- DON'T adjust to the airline meal service.
    (A false social **cycle**.)

5) ATMOSPHERE:

A) Get your **feet** up after **takeoff**:
- to take pressure off your lumbars.
- to cushion engine vibration.
- to enhance blood circulation.

B) Coping strategy for **dehydration**:
- drink 8-16 fl. oz. liquid per hour of travel time.
- request full bottle/can purified **water** each service.
- breathe through moistened **hanky**.
- mist face with atomizer.
- **oil** nostrils.
- moisturize around **eye**s/any exposed skin.

C) Coping strategy for thin/stuffy air:
- twist/tilt gasper **airvent** (blower) to suit.
- practice **conscious breathing**.
- ask **attendant** for **oxygen**.

6) **LAV**S:

A) Wear **shoes**.
    (The floor is invariably puddled.)

B) Avoid contamination.
    (Wash hands with hot water/soap.)

7) **EXERCISE**:

   A) **Conscious breathing**:
   - inhale/exhale to balanced count.

   B) **Groucho walk**:
   - circuit the plane with bent knees, straight back.

   C) Let body lead:
   - raise arms, pinwheels, etc.

8) **SUBTLE ENERGY**:

   A) Takeoff:
   - light-headed opportunity to dream state.
   - cast off old **fear**s.

   B) Metaphysical **exercise**:
   - swim, jog, your pleasure.

   C) **Aspecting**:
   - use clouds to communicate with subconscious.

   D) **Telepathy**:
   - connect with beloveds on Earth.

9) DESCENT:

   A) Anything on board **inoperative**?
   - tell **attendant.**

   B) **Ear**s hurt during descent?
   - yawn, swallow, harden tongue, blow out.
   - steam-heat.
   - inform **attendant.**

   C) Feeling ill or unduly **fatigue**d?
   - request **wheelchair** from attendant.
           (The **pilot** will radio ahead; no charge.)

JET DOWN
(Immigration, **Customs**, **Baggage Claim**)

1) DISEMBARKATION:

    A) Pay attention:
- be careful *schlepping* **luggage** after inactivity.
- look both ways on airstrip (if no jetway).

    B) What to do during **transit**:
- aerobic **exercise**.
- stretches.
- **conscious breathing**.
- stroll to the beat of own pulse.
- sightsee.
- **meditate**.

2) **CUSTOMS**:

    Expedite customs clearance:
- accessorize clothing.
- lean towards agent.
- sneeze!

3) **BAGGAGE CLAIM**:

    A) Have claim tags ready.

    B) Watch out for pushy people with bashing bags.

4) **AIRPORT** SERVICES:

    Information booth tip:
- ask for a note stating your destination in local language.
- pin it to your shirt.

5) **SUBTLE ENERGY**:

    Pay attention to inner self orientation.

JET LET-GO
(Car/Taxi/Bus/Rail Away from **Airport**)

1) EXIT **AIRPORT** TERMINAL:

A) Arrival tip:
- if no checked bags and you are being met
avoid crowds/auto fumes
rendezvous outside Departures.

B) **Cold-weather** formula:
- **niacin**.
- deep-heat rub.
- longjohns.

2) **SUBTLE ENERGY**:

A) Visual **grounding**:
- observe shift from old to new world.
- immerse in local **light**, as if impressionist painting.

B) Auditory grounding:
- hear ambient sound.
- listen for the unheard sounds.
(The rhythms/speeds of local social **cycles**.)

C) Touch grounding:
- embrace family/friends at **airport**.
- linger in a hug, hold hands.

D) Scent grounding:
- inhale scent of local-grown **flowers**.
- notice ambient scents.

E) Relax:
- recall a love felt before.
- give yourself the gift of that love again.

JETLAG
(Coping with that Taxing **Time** Warp)

1) **WATER**:

   A) Drink a gallon a day for three days post-flight:
- flush.   - rehydrate.
- vitalize body's own electrical charge.

   B) Submerge ASAP!
- swim/bathe in ocean/river/pool/tub.
- a minimum of ten minutes in water.
- be held and floated:
  - clockwise in **Northern Hemisphere.**
  - counterclockwise in **Southern**.

   C) Therapeutic **bath**:
1 - salt/baking soda.
2 - submerge.
3 - drain **jetlag**.
4 - cold **shower**.

2) DIET:

   A) Break **fast** with watery foods
           (soup/fruit/vegetables).

   B) Local-grown food accelerates acclimatization.

   C) Neutralize **radiation** with:
- high-**chlorophyll** foods
        (spinach/chard/kale/seaweed).
- SOD.

3) **EXERCISE**:

   A) Stretch:
- to accelerate adaptability.

   B) Aerobic:
- jog/dance/tennis/whatever you enjoy most.

C) Nature **walk**:
- provides exercise AND
- informs the mind AND
- orients the cells to local **light**.

4) UNPACK:

A) Clean outside of **luggage** first.

B) Update your permanent packing checklist.

C) Store **valuables**:
- in zippered case in hotel safe.
- in bag secured with combination lock.

5) **SLEEP**:

A) Resist your old sleep time.
>   (If exhausted a.m., take short nap only.)

B) Before sleep:
- practice **conscious breathing**.
- stretch.
- visualize and affirm.

C) How to sleep when you're not tired:
1 - Eat your main meal.
2 - Take a hot bath.
3 - Darken the room.
4 - Cover the windows of the body (**eyes**, **ears**).
5 - Practice determination.
6 - Split consciousness, then merge them.

6) POST-FLIGHT AWARENESS:

A) Stepping out in foreign land:
- take hotel name in local language.
>   (Matchbook!)

B) IF YOU:

1 - Catch a respiratory illness within two weeks,
2 - Become seriously ill,
3 - Feel that your jet was in poor repair,

THEN YOU SHOULD NOTIFY:
- the airline.
- your newspaper.
- Congress.
- ASI.

INCLUDE WITH YOUR NOTIFICATION:
- flight number/date.
- aircraft number.
- sector flown.
- date of illness.

7) **SUBTLE ENERGY**:

A) About going to work:
- rest first.
- after **east**bound flights, evenings are best.
- after flying **west**, mornings are best.

B) **Bodywork** and **skin brushing**:
- restore vitality.
- release endorphins.
- remove static accumulated en route.

C) Tune into:
- words.
- **symptoms**/signals.
- body language.
- **climate**.
- Cosmic **cycle**s.
- social cycles.

D) Keep your attitude:
- positive.
- child-like.
- REMEMBER, have fun.
        (**Time** flies when you're having fun.)

ORDERING

If JET SMART is not yet available at your local bookstore and/or if you want to participate in our survey, contact the publisher:

FLYANA RHYME Inc - PO Box 300
Makawao, Maui, Hawaii 96768 - USA
Tel/FAX 808.572.5252

For a copy of JET SMART please send U.S. $12.95 (check or money order) plus the appropriate shipping charge:

$2.00 in the United States $4.00 Europe/South America

$2.50 Canada/Mexico $5.50 Asia/Africa/Pacific Rim

For information on diodes and other recommended products please call or write for a catalog.

YOUR NAME_____

STREET ADDRESS_____

CITY, STATE, ZIP_____

TOTAL ENCLOSED: $12.95 +_____=_____

SURVEY

The best thing about flying is:

The first thing which needs to be changed about flying is:

My synonym for jetlag (in five words or less) is:

How many flights (roundtrips count 2) have you taken in your life?